# Introductory Concepts in
# Information Science

# Introductory Concepts in
# Information Science

## Melanie J. Norton

WITHDRAWN

*asis*

**ASIS Monograph Series**

Published for the
American Society for Information Science by

**Information Today, Inc.**
**Medford, New Jersey**

Third Printing, January 2004

*Introductory Concepts in Information Science*

**Library of Congress Cataloging-in-Publication Data**

Introductory concepts in information science / edited by Melanie J. Norton.
     p. cm. — (ASIS monograph series)
  Includes bibliographical references and index.
  ISBN 1-57387-087-0
   1. Information science. I. Norton, Melanie. II. Series.

Z665 .I67 2000
020—dc21

                      99-462193

Publisher: Thomas H. Hogan, Sr.
Editor-in-Chief: John B. Bryans
Managing Editor: Janet M. Spavlik
Production Manager: M. Heide Dengler
Copy Editor: Diane Zelley
Cover Designer: Adam Vinick
Book Designer: Trejo Production, Princeton, NJ
Indexer: Laurie Andriot

# Table of Contents

# Introduction

It is not the intention here to attempt a definitive declaration of what information or information science is, but rather to stimulate a constructive and creative discourse upon both topics. An open mind and an open hand will serve as better aids in examining these complex topics than any endeavor at straitjacket definitions. This introduction to concepts in information science offers ideas, issues, examples, and projections to begin the long process of investigating the topics. It is not possible, in a reasonably sized volume, to present all the ideas, concerns, and aspects of information and information science; hence, this work is not represented as being more than an introduction.

Choices had to be made about inclusion and exclusion, depth, scope, and so on. An introduction to information as a concept and information science as a field comprise the first two chapters. Within Chapter Two are also included two reprinted articles, one from Harold Borko and one from Otten and Debons, that give perspectives on information science. Communication as a process closely related to information in a number of ways is discussed in Chapter Three. Information retrieval as a concept and activity is covered in Chapter Four. Chapter Five introduces and describes bibliometrics, and Chapter Six brings out the information economy, the underlying rationale for the emerging criticality of information. A discussion of the concepts of information value is presented in Chapter Seven, and Chapter Eight, co-authored by my colleague June Lester, presents an exploration of the impact of information technology on the information hierarchy.

This text is an attempt to provide a place to begin. The direction one travels after that will be the reader's path of interest and interpretation with my hope that this beginning study of information and information science provides a modest light by which to investigate these areas further.

# Chapter 1

# Information and Information Science

## Introduction

Information science has deep historical roots accented with significant controversy and conflicting views. The concepts of this science may be at the heart of many disciplines, but the emergence of a specific discipline of information science has been limited to the twentieth century. Protracted discussion of the definition of information, knowledge, communication, and uncertainty have created insight into the complexities of human information behaviors and the information scientist may be the best demonstrator of the science. While gaining recognition that this thing, "information," may play critical roles in our social and intellectual activities, we have overlooked the result of the depth of its integration into our existence and neglected to realize its impact upon us in the study of it. As we have gained information and formed knowledge about the topic, we have ignored how such progress does alter our knowledge base. While studying the thing that changes us most, we have become resistant to the notion of change in our view of it.

This chapter presents a grandiose view of information to encourage the discussion of information in all its possible roles as well as a brief historical foundation of information science to provide some location in time for this discussion. The foundation is not comprehensive, that would be a volume in and of itself, but it highlights some situations and people that contributed to the development of information science today. As there are many disciplines that contribute to this field, it is not possible to identify all the key figures.

## The Grandest View of Information and Information Science

What one should recognize about information science is that it is a study that reflects the accumulation of events and thought springing from humankind's information hunger. As we strive to better understand the world that surrounds us, and to control it, we have a voracious appetite for information. We also crave to understand this component of ourselves and our world—information, and information hunger. As such, many fields have and will continue to contribute to improving our understanding of this aspect of our character and the implications of its transformations upon us.

If information science is concerned with all aspects, properties, and behaviors of information, as suggested by Borko's synthesis of Robert S. Taylor's three definitions of information science (Borko, 1968), then it certainly involves all disciplines at some level. Information could actually be construed as "existing" back to the first exchange or recombination of chemicals in the primordial ooze. Though the image may seem exaggerated, it does suggest the depth and scope of information as an element in our existence, from birth to death and across the generations. The study of information, its aspects, behaviors, and properties could theoretically have begun prior to clay tablets and papyrus. The case could be made that early philosophers were seeking to understand information as they attempted to derive meaning from the world (Debons, 1990). It does not appear farfetched to consider that observations of daily life are a form of information gathering, exchange, and implementation; it seems almost too fundamental to consider. Do observations qualify as science? This also is open to debate. In discussing prescientific times, Heilprin comments, referring to Plato's conclusions that our senses could not be relied upon, "It took centuries of mostly celestial observations by great thinkers such as Copernicus and Galileo to render sense perception acceptable" (1995, p. 575). Forms of observation have been the basis of most early science. Consider Newton, Darwin, or Mendel, as well as Copernicus and Galileo—it was what they observed, as well as what they interpreted the observations to be, which formed the basis for further exploration and developing knowledge. Where would science be without the observations and mental work of these early scientists? The observations, the transactions, the implementation of behaviors may be the subjects of study and reveal that information, at some level in the social or physical organism, "forms the very basis of life" (Debons et al., 1988, p. 9). Information has been compared to energy and matter, as a fundamental element (Otten and Debons, 1970).

The science, the efforts to understand and study information, came long after the observations of information began. If information science studies and investigates all the properties, aspects, and behavior of information, then it is concerned at some point with virtually everything known, thought, considered, espoused, and imagined. If one limits the definition to "recorded" information, the topic becomes more manageable but much less reflective of the formation of information and the characteristics that influence much of its interpretation and handling. Information is not bound to one medium of transport and is not limited to one form of expression, or even interpretation. "What is information?" is the question that bedevils. Information is some essential aspect of our existence that we have yet to be completely comfortable explaining. Our understanding of our total environment—physical, emotional, intellectual, current and historical—is perpetually changing. As information seems to be the thread that links us to everything else, it would make sense that as our perception of knowledge changes, so too should our sense of information. Information is more than recorded words and languages; it is images, music, light, any entity that interacts as largely as in concert with the universe or as minutely as subatomic particles. Information is something around us all the time, something we also create, accumulate, evaluate, manipulate, consume, and integrate. It is something we ignore, are not conscious of at all times, and do not always accept or integrate.

As you read these words, there is an enormous number of sources of information available to you, consciously and unconsciously. Your body is receiving information about the room you are in, the level of light, the room temperature, humidity, and airflow. Your body may also be receiving information about the color of the walls, the previous occupants of the room (via odors, dander, and such). Your body is working with this information, generally without your awareness until the information has some unusual impact upon your system, such as overheating, allergic reaction, chills—all responses to information your body is receiving. At the point you become conscious of the information, you may decide to ignore it or consciously react. Due to physical limitations, you may not be able to exert any control over your body's interpretation of the information and its reactions, such as perspiring, sneezing, raising a rash or goose bumps, or worse—all from information you were possibly not conscious of receiving or sending.

It seems obvious that information is an essential element in the formation of all things, whether societies, human beings, or sciences. All that we are has been built on the previous use of information to create our societies, our cultures, religions, machines, and knowledge. So information science is the study of all of these, at least in some respect. There are characteristics about this progression that require some mention. It has taken thousands of years of evolution of humanity and cultures to reach today. Puzzling out the meaning of life has sometimes been no more than trying to survive. Making sense of the dark and the day, and the changing seasons, developing group identity, defining the boundaries for hunting and gathering, all these took time, much longer than any of us will ever live or imagine accurately. Each small piece of information that had some value, or supposed value was kept and passed on, sometimes building upon previous information. Much information was also missed, not gathered, not retained, not believed. As one group warred with and destroyed another, all too often the information and knowledge of the defeated group was lost. The truth is that the complexity of understanding how early humankind came to interpret the universe around them is beyond our comprehension. Today, we are born into a world filled with more information, more conflict, more structure than any of our predecessors. We cannot imagine not having a past, just as we cannot readily grasp the future. Somehow, humanity examined the world in which it lived and began to develop mechanisms to cope with the unexplainable, which involved almost everything for many centuries. Curiosity and observation led to possible explanations, impossible stories, and entrenched beliefs.

New tools have expanded our vision and our horizons. Telescopes, satellites, space vehicles help us to look not just beyond the edge of the map, but lightyears away into time. What we see of the sky now is light from history; the distance is so great that by the time we have perceived it, the stars and the planets have already lived millions of years and are actually no longer in the sky where we see them. The boundaries of our senses have been expanded and our access to information limited only by time and imagination.

Information is an all-pervasive creature available at many levels, in previously unimaginable forms, in overwhelming quantity. Short of death, there is no escape from the need for information and no respite from the profusion of information. As populations grew, as our society became more complex, the production and perceived needs for information expanded. As new mediums became available for transporting information, new forms of information became transportable and more information was demanded, which required more ways of transporting it. Such has been the behavior of information production and information need.

New technology has enhanced the effect exponentially. Discovering new methods of storing and retrieving information led to new methods of acquiring information. These new abilities to handle information contributed to the increase of information. With the perception, if not the reality, that more information could be handled, there grew the notion that more is needed. Attendant upon this information combustion, there have been changes wrought by its influx. Where once we glanced out the window to check the weather, we now turn on a radio, television, or computer to obtain forecasts of the weather, and we hope for longer sight into the day. Once we sought only familial sources of advice; we now delve deeply into self-help information—available at every bookstand, radio station, newspaper, and television channel, in Web chat rooms, and from anonymous electronic friends we never meet except in cyberspace. Our living rooms are not just gathering places for friends and family but for the combined powers of an entire industry of entertainment, news, marketing, and gospel. Our home computers allow another whole world of people and ideas into our lives that we might never have experienced otherwise. We have access to information in quantities and forms previously unknown. Information technology makes it possible to interact with anyone else who has technology access. The barriers of time become our personal time constraints and the bandwidth available.

Information employed and embedded into a context, integrated as it were, may become what we call knowledge. To know something is to possess information, but having information affect in some way what we know, or believe, may be construed as knowledge. Developing knowledge may be a cumulative affair, involving the acquisition of information over time to have a meaningful effect (Buckland, 1991). Using information as building blocks may result in knowledge, sometimes held as truth, regardless of the validity of the assumption, and sometimes denied as heresy. Galileo observed "new" stars with his telescope, which no naked eye could detect. That information was out there, available, but not detected, not part of a belief system, not an "accepted" part of current knowledge, and not part of Galileo's belief either (Boorstin, 1983). Buckland reasons that belief is an important aspect of knowledge, not whether something is true or false but whether it is believed. The telescope itself, which Galileo improved upon, was a building block, as it was the result of an idea of another fellow. Examining the sky, the stars and planets, Galileo reasoned that Copernicus' theory of some fifty years prior, that the Earth could not be the center of the universe, might be valid. This was contrary to his belief and the accepted knowledge of his time (Boorstin).

The particulars of how each society over time managed information would be a fascinating discussion, but is not appropriate here. Nor is it appropriate to explore at length the presence of information at all levels of existence, not just as an aspect of the human condition. The focus here shall be primarily on information in the human domain of control. To begin, one should recognize that information existed and was used, compiled, and applied long before the word was framed, and before anyone studied it. There is a relationship among information, knowledge, and belief (Buckland, 1991). So then, what does it involve, this study of information? It is the study of all the aspects of information's behavior and all that may impact information, its uses, its representations, and its applications (Borko, 1968). As we have gained information about information we have recognized that the scope of the study, the science, is much wider than earlier imagined. To study information one might study social systems, human interactions, cognition, language, literature, art forms, technology, history; essentially, any of the representations of information or knowledge, whether verbal, visual, imprinted, or electronically preserved, and how humans interact with these aspects. This is not to suggest that information and knowledge are equivalent; there is a relationship between them. Sometimes information provides fuel for knowledge, and vice versa, but do not think they are one and the same. It is not sound reasoning to assume because ideas or stories are in print that they are "true," nor should we assume all information, or knowledge, is necessarily "true." Information assumes various characters and roles, it is an economic entity, a precursor or cause to knowledge, a process, a thing in and of itself (Buckland), a component in virtually all transactions and surely other states or beings as yet unknown. As Buckland points out, and as we too shall subscribe, "We are unable to say confidently of anything that it could not be information" (p. 50).

Generally, one examines information science in the context of at least the following five areas: collection and storage; classification and control; access for retrieval; communication; and evaluation. How should decisions about what information to collect be made and once made how should it be stored? Related to storage is classification and control. Our predecessors recognized that some system of classification or organization of information could make it possible to discover more about the world and retrieve what was known, implying that classification is closely related to retrieval. Being able to select an item of information from a body of information involves the tasks labeled as retrieval. Communication is all the processes involved in the conveyance of information via many possible channels and with some very interesting complications. Evaluation is immediately noticed as being multilayered, in that there is an evaluation performed to collect information, an evaluation that may be performed on information to extract other information, and evaluation performed to retrieve information once stored. With time and experience it has become clear that there are cognitive sciences involved with all five of the above contexts, components of user behavior and involvement that dramatically impact information. The evolution of information technology—telegraph, telephone, radio, television, and the Internet—also have all come into consideration in the five contexts of information science. A maturing in academic valuation of the diversity of cultures requires that social actions, reactions, and impacts be considered in the field. Information may cause change, and change should affect information science.

Information science is the study of this multifaceted and hydra-headed enigma. At this point in time the primary considerations in this study focus on developing theories, empirical laws, or practical understandings and applications that may be applicable to information, its roles, behaviors, or influences (Borko, 1968). The study engages members of many disciplines ranging from library, computer, and cognitive sciences to sociology, economics, and statistics. In essence, there is no discipline that should not be investigating information in its implications to itself. Members of a diverse group of disciplines are studying information as information scientists, and they are producing generalizable results (Rayward, 1983). However, there will always be need for discipline perspectives and applications of information, which may not be revealed through generic research.

## Historical Foundations

### Evolving Views

Information science has roots in a variety of disciplines and fields. Inquiry into the history of information science reveals conflicting views as to its origins; its relationships to librarianship, scholarship, various disciplines; and the documentationalist movement. There have been those who would argue that the study of information is not a "science." Such debate has been long-winded and not particularly rewarding (Machlup and Mansfield, 1983; Machlup, 1983). Machlup makes the case that the meaning of "science" has changed over time, usually in an exclusionary manner, as advocates of specific interpretations attempted to diminish the status of those who held different views. He postulated that this habit was a method of equalizing and then enhancing each group's sense of superiority over the now excluded group. Equally unsatisfying has been the debate whether information science is a discipline, a subset of librarianship, an offspring of documentationalism, or a metadiscipline. This is not to imply that such discussion is not warranted; in fact, it is a necessary component of the development of the field and the declaration of its history, all of which are important. However, it is often presented as negative debate attempting much the same exclusiveness that Machlup discussed relevant to the discourse about science. It seems an awkward approach to an exciting and incredibly involved area of human endeavor to focus on all the disagreements and posturing. Kochen (1983) viewed the dispute over what discipline information studies falls into as fruitless semantic arguments. Plainly, more value would come from allowing those identified with the information disciplines to pursue the inquiry, seeking to improve our understanding. We will accept, at least for ease of this discourse, that information science is a science and it has potential contributors from virtually every field of study, every discipline, and every practicing profession (Borko, 1968; Machlup and Mansfield; Meadows, 1987). This does not relieve information scientists of the necessity to lay a foundation and invoke some of the mentioned conflicting views.

Perhaps some of the conflict results from the evolving nature of this "science," coupled with our own intellectual evolution. Before the printed book, the high science of memory, which allowed the retelling of history, laws, and even of early manuscript contents, required the teller to be present. The oral tradition was more than storytelling for entertainment, it was a way of transmitting information, education, moral plays, and cultural identity, but it was dependent upon the skills and availability of the human host (Boorstin, 1983). The preliterate traditions were linked to human carriers; faithfulness to completeness and accuracy in the rendition of the information was critical, as well as considered a sacred duty and much admired skill (Riesman, 1960). The development of new tools influenced the ability to share information and also decreased the reliance on the human memory (Boorstin). The development of writing, even in a pictorial form, was a method for preserving what was seen or occurred, and allowed it to be shared with others, without requiring both parties to be in the same place at the same time. Examples would be cave paintings in France, clay tablets from the Middle East, the pottery of the native Americans, the hand-scripted manuscripts of the Middle Ages. All of these permit the sharing of information, and indeed are themselves information as well as carriers, without requiring a human host, and often surviving the originating community (Riesman). Could not the ability to share information, to potentially influence others, contribute to an expanding view and understanding, altering what was viewed as information, even what was considered knowledge and truth? As information was more widely exchanged, it challenged beliefs and the accepted knowledge systems. If what we study is something that may cause significant change, then will not our study of it change, too? As we investigate information, should not our knowledge systems be challenged and changed? Is the study of medicine in this decade the identical study of medicine three decades ago? Why should the study of information remain as narrow as its original interpretation? Is it immune to the effects of its mission?

Perhaps most simply, the issue is change and our resistance to it. As elders bemoan the unworthiness of their offspring, especially as the young dispense with that which the elder once prized, perhaps that is the root of the problem in conflicts surrounding information science. It is by necessity responsive to changes in the environment; the knowledge base grows and technology evolves, the new information science is applied to the old and change occurs.

## Previous Considerations

Early scholars were plagued by the political turmoil of their times, sometimes forced into silence about their discoveries, frequently secretive about their work, sharing it with only a limited number of colleagues to ensure their primacy and safety (Boorstin, 1983). Letter writing as a method of communication among interested scientists was the early distributor of discovery. Letters were more difficult to censor than books because it was easier to hide them, and if the document was not hidden the phrasing could well be structured to conceal ideas as mere discussion. In later times, when politically acceptable and appropriately rewritten, letters discussing observations or discoveries would be published (Boorstin).

The printing press expanded the availability of information by making it possible to create more than one copy of a document in an economy of time. It was no longer necessary to hand copy each document, making information available to a far wider audience than any previous tool. The growth in volume of "knowledge" created a crisis of access and communication. The need to share ideas more effectively, to better expand the universe of knowledge, and frankly, to protect an individual's claim to a new idea led to publications of scholarly letters, then papers. The awarding of prizes for discovery and the attainment of a certain celebrity caused significant competition to be identified with a discovery (Boorstin, 1983). Eventually collections of papers became journals, which produced new concerns—how to access the information in an economical and useful manner. Growth in the production of scientific works and the printed record created problems of access and discovery, often causing important information to be overlooked. Bernal (1939) suggested that if a solution to the organization of scientific communications was not resolved soon, more knowledge would be lost than was gained (Meadows, 1987).

One of the promulgators of modern information science was the "explosion" of recorded material in the nineteenth century coupled with a lack of adequate systems to access the material. A pioneer in bibliographic construction and a wide variety of related endeavors, Paul Otlet, a Belgium lawyer in the 1890s, would significantly contribute to addressing those difficulties and be credited as the originator of the documentalist movement in Europe (Rayward, 1997). In the early 1890s in Brussels, Belgium, Paul Otlet, working with Henri La Fontaine, began to contemplate new ways of making printed text accessible via the creation of a bibliography of all printed material. He envisioned a method of representing subject contents of printed material on cards, which could then be grouped to simulate the relationships involved. Otlet sought a method to classify knowledge to implement the proper ordering of the cards. After encountering a copy of Dewey's Decimal Classification system, Otlet and La Fontaine became convinced, and convinced others, it should be possible to create a "universal catalog of all knowledge" (p. 291). Ultimately, an association of interested parties would lead to the formation of the International Institute of Bibliography (IIB), which would be the International Office of Bibliography in Brussels (IOB). The IIB/IOB would be the repository for the catalog to be built. Over time the IIB/IOB became the current International Federation for Information and Documentation (Rayward).

Using a much expanded version of the Dewey Decimal Classification (DDC) system, the Classification Decimale Universelle or UDC (Universal Decimal Classification) was initiated in 1895. This was the scheme to organize all knowledge and the basis for organization of the subject cards. The UDC expanded upon and increased the flexibility of its antecedent DDC. The UDC structure was based on a bibliography, a subject index that permits classification of portions of materials (Foskett, 1966; McIlwaine, 1997). Rayward likens the UDC to a database management system. The UDC employed what became a complex, numerically based series of codes that were intended to represent the structures and substructures of classification relevant to a particular entry. The complexity of the numeric system and the attempt to provide associations among related items made the system too intricate for the technology of the time to fully utilize. Otlet significantly addressed some of the shortcomings of the card and cabinet database; he developed the notion of standardizing card sizes and entries, and employing colors as well as minor card size variations to contribute to the organization of the catalog and to improve the speed of searching by providing a visual structure to the database. Despite the problems of the time, the catalog, the Repertorie Bibliographique Universel (RBU), begun in 1895, would grow to almost sixteen million entries by 1930. Other databases were created based on the same premise as the RBU and to supplement it. This included an image database and a "multimedia" collection of pamphlets, brochures, and hand copied passages.

The actual manual tasks of handling the catalogs proved difficult. Early attempts at providing database search services entailed locating the appropriate cards, hand copying entries and refiling, which was time-intensive and tended to introduce errors both in the copied material and during refiling. However, searches were performed; users were instructed in the proper phrasing applying the UDC numbers so the staff could locate the appropriate entries in the database and copy the card (Rayward, 1997). Rayward believes that Otlet and La Fontaine were engaged in activities and intellectual endeavors, such as database construction (the UDC and card collection), information retrieval, and developing search strategies that today would be encompassed under information science.

In 1903, Otlet devised the word "documentation" (Williams, 1997) to describe the intellectual and actual processes of bringing together for application "all the written or graphic sources of our knowledge . . . " (Rayward, 1997, p. 299). His interest included the processes in the creation of the content of works; their collection; the analysis to describe them in detail; and the dissection of the physical material into its subject components so that the parts could be placed together in relationship to similar materials to create a documentary file. Lastly, all the novel aspects of each work would essentially be classified to become part of a larger overall delineation of science (Rayward). In the context of his time, Otlet was interested in the organization, storage, and retrieval of information in all the forms in which it is preserved as well as in the intellectual and practical concerns of the tasks involved. His vision included the technology of the time and anticipated its improvement and continued application. The UDC system he devised continues to be used today in French-speaking parts of Europe, Africa, and Latin America as well as in some special libraries in English-speaking countries (McIlwaine, 1997, p. 331).

Rayward (1997) credits Otlet for proposing the device that H. G. Wells would later describe as a "World Brain" and Vannevar Bush would designate as Memex. Indeed, what was viewed as rather wild mental gymnastics in 1903, 1938, and 1945, respectively, has taken form in the latter part of the century. In 1945, *Atlantic Monthly* published "As We May Think" by Vannevar Bush. As director of the Office of Scientific Research and Development for the United States, Bush had coordinated the efforts of American scientists during World War II to apply science to warfare. Looking toward the end of the war, Bush urged scientific efforts be focused on making knowledge accessible (reprinted in Meadows, 1987). Bush proposed, among other things, a device that could act as a supplement to the human brain, which would permit the acquisition of knowledge from a storage unit without the cumbersome indexes of the time, but rather by a manner of association, quickly, efficiently (Meadows). It could be construed that he was proposing a modern computer, perhaps a computer connected to a network, which permitted the selection of information via association and via relationships. While speed or efficiency of networks or Web searches are relative and could be debated, there can be no question that compared to the systems in use in 1945, the current devices are phenomenal. Over time we learn and apply what we learn, building on previous information and knowledge. (The serious student of information science would be well served to read both Vannevar Bush's "As We Might

Think," and a later related work, "Memex Revisited," written in 1967.) Bush's work motivated a renewed interest in information storage, transmission, and access by a variety of disciplines (Debons, 1990). It is significant that Bush's work is still cited in reference to having a role in information science and computer science.

Warfare was another important contributor to interest in what is now known as information science and why it is by necessity a study involving many disciplines. World War II created demand for scientific information to combat the military technology and advantage of Germany and Japan. The depth of the Great Depression of 1929 had devastated the scientific efforts in all but government-sponsored situations prior to the attack on Pearl Harbor. The war gave real motivation and impetus toward invigorating the research apparatus of this country. Technological research involved communications, cryptography, detection systems such as sonar and radar, weaponry, delivery systems, manufacturing, computers, and more. Materials, even food, were rationed, not just due to supply transport problems, but to divert these goods or raw materials to the war effort. Significant research efforts were undertaken, one of the most famous being the Manhattan project, the atomic weapon research that ultimately ended the war in the Pacific. The Cold War also contributed to renewed interest in technology and science to prevent the United States from falling behind the Soviet bloc in developing technology. The launching of Sputnik by the Soviets shocked the United States and spurred a renewed interest in science and scientific communication and information, as well as in the generation of knowledge. The Cuban Missile Crisis of the early 1960s fueled United States' concerns about Soviet military prowess. The presence of a serious nuclear missile threat a mere ninety miles off the coast of the United States emphasized the importance of advancing technologic knowledge, which required investigation into the creation, transfer, and behavior of information and knowledge. Military considerations continued to fuel interest in developing more advanced methods of handling and managing information, with some emphasis on the perspective of computer information and data processing, as these devices are critical to the management of certain weapon systems. Space exploration significantly influenced the increased concern with information management systems, computer communications, human behavior in relation to technology, artificial intelligence, expert systems, and much more (Debons, 1990).

## Association Trails

Professional or scholarly organizations usually attract people with related interests, typically common problems, challenges, or aspirations. These organizations are often the providers and consumers of their own research, because the organization addresses issues in their realm of curiosity (Pearce, 1993; Norton, 1998). Theoretically, these associations can also be indicative of movement and development of specialties or disciplines (Crane, 1972). Williams (1997) argues that the Special Library Association (SLA) held interests more closely affiliated to the documentalist Otlet than with the American Library Association (ALA), which was the professional organization of librarians and the group from which SLA emerged in 1909. The focus of members of the SLA was to provide for the specific information needs of their organizations' users, regardless of format. SLA members were in situations that could not be generalized under the traditional library model of the time. Their concerns included the entire information process for their particular users, and usually involved formats or materials that would not be handled in other types of libraries.

In 1937, the American Documentation Institute (ADI) was formed, heavily influenced by the 1935 Congress of the International Institute of Documentation (Williams, 1997). SLA became one of ADI's sponsors, but ADI interests, while related to SLA's, were more general. ADI had a more national perspective, it associated with the larger research and governmental projects and therefore had less specifically focused concerns than SLA. Prior to World War II, the ADI was more oriented to dissemination of information, and not particularly on acquisition, or user services, both issues of importance to SLA. However, their interests were more aligned than SLA felt (Williams). Shera (1966) suggests that traditional librarianship in this country, as represented by ALA, became involved in the "cult of universal education and self-improvement," to the detriment of some professional growth. Documentalists and SLA were open to undertake the development of new technologies and the extension of traditional library tools to new materials. Interpretations of these alliances would be best left to the historical participants. Suffice it to say some significant ideological differences prevented the three organizations from becoming one. The division of thought placed SLA and ADI closer and more cooperative with one another than with ALA, despite the underlying foundational interests of all three being essentially the same: "1) acquisition of *appropriate* materials, and 2) their organization and interpretation for effective use" (Shera, 1966, p. 48). While the application of the material, the special circumstances of handling various formats, and the separate missions of the institutes that members of these three associations serve may differ, they are all associations interested in information as a practical and theoretical concern. The speed at which they adapted emerging technology to address their concerns, or the willingness to experiment with different methodologies is no more significant to their profession than it is in general society and business. Different people, organizations, businesses, and institutions approached information technology at different speeds with widely varying success.

In 1968, the ADI changed its name to the American Society for Information Science (ASIS). Its membership included SLA and ALA members, but also a wide variety of science and technology disciplines and even some that might be positioned in the humanities. Taking a multi- and interdisciplinary approach to information concerns has yielded a richer, more diverse research front. The diversity of contributors has applied novel methods to the investigation while providing improved or new approaches to the practical problems of information organization, manipulation, and access in a wider arena (Rayward, 1983).

There is no small irony that at the writing of this volume there is an enlarging debate in the library and information science community about librarianship, documentation, and information science in all of its possible configurations. In April 1999, the ALA sponsored a series of online discussion topics and a national meeting, the Congress on Professional Education (online), to examine the roles and educational criteria for the library professional. Among many issues of concern were the implications of name changes and potentially related curricular changes at the professional education institutions, where library may be removed from the title of the program. Concerns regarding the instruction of core competencies, such as cataloging, have been raised. The appearance of conflict among the accrediting body and the educational institutions has stirred a movement to discuss and clarify the role of the library and information professionals and educators via a series of interactions and contacts. The ongoing nature of the debate about information science continues to feed upon itself and its practitioners. As both Borko (1968) and Debons (1970) point out, there must be bridges between theory and practice, application and research. The field is a growing, changing entity that requires the attention and participation of all who are willing to expand their horizons. Information science involves many disciplines and practitioners, with slightly differing foci and concerns. Continued advances in technology and the study of information from all its various aspects will ensure unprecedented transformations in information science and all the related professions. As our understanding of information and its effects on all elements of our lives develops, we will be forced into accepting new professional roles and responsibilities in order to remain competitive.

## Summary

Information is the fundamental link among all that we are, know, and do not know. Attempting to understand all the ramifications of information is an increasingly involved and complex collection of practical and research activities. As more is discovered about information and information behaviors, the more there is yet to discover.

Information science has a much debated and tangled history. It can be demonstrated that theories and concerns currently identified as information science topics were at issue for the earliest scholars (Weinberg, 1997). Even when most information was transmitted by human carrier via memory, the issue of storage and information transfer was real (Reisman, 1960). The concerns for access to information were not decreased by the development of the printing press. If anything, the printing press created even more demand for the investigation of collection and storage, classification, retrieval, communication, and evaluation. More complex techniques had to be devised to provide for more complex document systems as well as an explosion of information. Otlet's documentalist notions are closely related to current concepts of information science and information provision, classification flexibility, and resources to access the interior subject content of documents of all formats. Otlet expanded the notion of information content to objects and graphics as well as attempting to include them in searchable systems. Applying Dewey's Decimal Classification, with modification, Otlet initiated a continuing experiment in classification. He also proposed, among many other things, what later would provide the basis for Bush's Memex, which in turn spurred tremendous growth in the research efforts down the path toward modern automation (Rayward, 1997).

Information science is a widening study that will continue to mature and fracture into specialties, if it is not yet doing so, and that is debatable too. Information is part of the world in which we live and work. Our ability to examine it and to develop an understanding of the roles and characters it plays will contribute to future knowledge. As more information is examined, more will be found. It is unlikely the complexity of the issue will diminish. As the impact of information influences all aspects of our existence, it is clear that the study is in its infancy, as is our comprehension of the magnitude of information as a phenomena.

# References

Bernal, J. D. 1939. Scientific Communication. In A. J. Meadows, (Ed.). 1987. *The Origins of Information Science* pp. 167–183. B. Cronin, (Series Ed.) Foundations of Information Science. vol. 1. London, UK: Taylor Graham.

Boorstin, D. J. 1983. *The Discovers.* Random House: New York.

Borko, H. January 1968. Information Science: What Is It? *American Documentation* 19(1):3–5.

Buckland, M. 1991. *Information and Information Systems.* Praeger: New York.

Crane, D. 1972. *Invisible Colleges: Diffusion of Knowledge in Scientific Communities.* Chicago: The University of Chicago Press.

Debons, A. 1990. Foundations of Information Science. In M. C. Yovits, (Ed.) *Advances in Computers* 31:325–371. Boston: Academic Press.

Debons, A., Horne, E. and Cronenweth, S. 1988. *Information Science: an Integrated View.* Boston, MA: G. K. Hall.

Foskett, D. J., (Ed.). 1966. *Documentation and the Organization of Knowledge.* By Shera, J. H. Hamden, CT: Archon Books.

Heilprin, L. B. 1995. Science and Technology: From Prescientific Times to the Present. *Journal of the American Society for Information Science* 46(8):574–578.

Kochen, M. 1983. Library Science and Information Science. In F. Machlup and U. Mansfield, (Eds.). *The Study of Information: Interdisciplinary Messages* pp. 371–377. New York: John Wiley & Sons.

Machlup, F. 1983. Semantic Quirks in Studies of Information. In F. Machlup and U. Mansfield, (Eds.). *The Study of Information: Interdisciplinary Messages* pp. 641–671. New York: John Wiley & Sons.

Machlup, F. and Mansfield, U., (Eds.) 1983. *The Study of Information: Interdisciplinary Messages.* New York: John Wiley & Sons.

McIlwaine, I. C. 1997. The Universal Decimal Classification: Some Factors Concerning Its Origins, Development, and Influence. *Journal of the American Society for Information Science* 48(4):331–339.

Meadows, A. J., (Ed.) 1987. *The Origins of Information Science.* B. Cronin, (Series Ed.) Foundations of Information Science. vol. 1. London, UK: Taylor Graham.

Norton, M. J. 1998. Volunteer and business organizations: Similar issues for collaboration. In *Proceedings of the 1998 American Society for Information Science Midyear Meeting. Orlando, FL. May 16–20, 1998* pp.78–83.

Olsgaad, J. N., (Ed.) 1989. *Principles and Applications of Information Science for Library Professionals.* Chicago: American Library Association.

Otten, K. and Debons, A. 1970. Opinion Paper. Towards a Metascience of Information: Informatology. *Journal of the American Society for Information Science* pp. 89–94.

Pearce, J. L. 1993. *Volunteers: The Organizational Behavior of Unpaid Workers.* New York, NY: Routledge.

Rapoport, A. 1953. What Is Information? *ETC: A Review of General Semantics* 10(4): 5–13. In T. Saracevic, (Ed.). 1970. *Introduction to Information Science.* New York: R. R. Bowker:5–12.

Rayward, B. W. 1983. Library and Information Sciences: Disciplinary Differentiation, Competition, and Convergence. In F. Machlup and U. Mansfield (Eds.). *The Study of Information: Interdisciplinary Messages* pp. 343–364 New York: John Wiley & Sons.

Rayward, B. W. 1997. The Origins of Information Science and the International Institute of Bibliography/International Federation for Information and Documentation (FID). *Journal of the American Society for Information Science* 48(4):289–300.

Riesman, D. 1960. The Oral and Written Traditions. In E. Carpenter and M. McLuhan, (Eds.) *Explorations in Communication* pp. 109–116. Beacon.

Shera, J. H. 1966. Documentation and the Organization of Knowledge. Foskett, D. J., (Ed). Hamden, CT: Archon Books.

Saracevic, T., (Ed.). 1970. *Introduction to Information Science*. New York: R. R. Bowker.

Taylor, R. S. 1966. Professional Aspects of Information Science and Technology. In C. A. Cuadra, (Ed.). *Annual Review of Information Science and Technology*. vol.1. New York: John Wiley & Sons.

Weinberg, B. H. 1997. The Earliest Hebrew Citation Indexes. *Journal of the American Society for Information Science* 48(4):318–330.

Williams, R.V. 1997. The Documentation and Special Libraries Movements in the United States, 1910–1960. *Journal of the American Society for Information Science* 48(9): 775–781.

# Chapter 2

# Two Perspectives on Information Science Reprinted

The discussion of what is information science and what role it will have in our world has been an ongoing debate for several decades. In 1968, Harold Borko, wishing to prepare an answer to inquiries about the meaning of the name change of the American Documentation Institute to the American Society for Information Science, wrote "Information Science: What Is it?" With his permission the entire paper is included here for review and discussion. Not so oddly, the question of what information science is, persists. Borko's remarks remain very pertinent if not slightly prophetic. As Eugene Garfield, who proposed and effected the name change from ADI to ASIS, is proposing another name change for the Society to the American Society for Information Science and Technology, once again the discussion emerges as one of conflict and interpretation. The emergence of significantly more complex technologic tools to implement information processing, the application of technology to a larger and larger arena of endeavor, the integration of information technology into the educational, cultural, and political landscape should make it clear there will be no escaping either the mechanisms of information as expressed by the technology, or the much larger and inclusive effect of information itself upon our societies.

Borko identified nine categories, based on those defined by (at that time) *Current Research and Development in Scientific Documentation*. These categories seem to still be representative of the areas of study in the field: information needs and uses; documentation creation and copying; language analysis; translation; abstracting, classification, coding and indexing; system design; analysis and evaluation; pattern recognition and adaptive systems. Though much expanded in the area of coverage in 1999 than in 1968, these categories still provide extensive coverage of information science.

Klause Otten and Anthony Debons in 1970 published an opinion paper, included here with permission, for review and discussion; it attempts to formulate information science as a metascience, a superscience from which a common framework could be devised for all the scientists and participants in the information science fields to work within. This paper depicts information as a commodity and a basic phenomenon, like energy, or matter, an entity in and of its own with many adjunct characteristics. It expands on the disciplinary inclusiveness of information science, drawing into it mathematics, computer science, engineering science, library science, psychology and linguistics. To what should be added are all the cognitive and social sciences, economics and physical sciences, basically, there is no discipline that is not impacted by information and its science. Debons and Otten disagree with this broad definition of information science: "Definitions of information science have been suggested that are all inclusive: as sciences concerned with all aspects of information. Our definition of metascience of information should clearly not be misunderstood as one of an all inclusive science. We view the metascience of information as a very specific science, concerned only with the foundations of information-related science and technologies and not concerned with the content of these specialized disciplines." (p. 117). But, as information is a component of everything, every science, it is obvious that information science is all-inclusive. It is in specific practice and specific context, however, that a refinement in information science has to be considered. Information in a nuclear reaction is not measured in the same context as information in a baseball game. Implementation of information available to analyze a DNA sample is not the same as analyzing a chess game; therefore, it may be reasonable to report information science as all-inclusive at a meta level; it is critical to recognize that like other metafields, there are contextually sensitive and essential differentiations to be made.

The two papers present a sound historical basis to begin the investigation of information and information science and obviously have colored the tone of this volume. While these papers were offered within an academic and scientific context, it is important to recognize that information has those aspects, but is pervasive, invasive, persistent, and resistant in all areas of endeavor. Information is the link. While it is possible to discuss the identification of laws, and try to characterize information in comparison to what is known, care should be taken. Information is the underlying aspect of everything, known and unknown. It is not merely the electronic energy associated with bits and computers. It is what is at the root of how everything, every cell, every object, every atom exists and continues to exist. It does influence everything in ways not even recognized. Information units are DNA, the messages to create and replicate cells; information units are electrochemical exchanges within brain cells across synapses; information can replace confusion, reduce uncertainty, create new uncertainty, and information about information is not a contradiction but a fact. In its complexity and its simplicity, information is the link to all that we are, as beings, as creatures in societies, as members of organizations, as units in a larger universe, and as single individual generators of information. Studying information is to determine more about it and how it affects not just our organizations and systems and technologies but how those things in reaction are affected by us.

---

# Information Science: What Is It?*

## H. Borko

*Information Systems Technology Staff System Development Corp., Santa Monica, California*

Reprinted with permission: *American Documentation*—January 1968, pp. 3–5.

In seeking a new sense of identity, we ask, in this article, the questions: What is information science? What does the information scientist do? Tentative answers to these questions are given in the hope of stimulating discussion that will help clarify the nature of our field and our work.

## Introduction

Now that the American Documentation Institute has voted to change its name to the American Society for Information Science, many of us have been forced to try to explain to friends and colleagues what information science is, what an information scientist does, and how all of this relates to librarianship and documentation. Those of us who have tried to make such explanations know that this is a difficult task. As an exercise I decided to prepare an answer to these questions at leisure rather than under the pressure of a direct inquiry. Let me state at the outset that I don't think I have *the answer*. It is hoped that this paper may provide a focus for discussion so that we can clarify our thinking and perhaps be more articulate about who we are and what we do.

## Definition

The term "information science" has been with us for some time. In his chapter on the "Professional Aspects of Information Science and Technology" (1) in the *Annual Review*, Robert S. Taylor provides three definitions of information science. These have many points in common as well as some

---

*This paper was prompted by the suggestion, made by ADI Headquarters to the members of ADI, that the diversity of members and interests of the organization would be better represented if the name of the society were changed to American Society for Information Science.

differences in emphasis. The definition that follows has been derived from a synthesis of these ideas.

*Information science* is that discipline that investigates the properties and behavior of information, the forces governing the flow of information, and the means of processing information for optimum accessibility and usability. It is concerned with that body of knowledge relating to the origination, collection, organization, storage, retrieval, interpretation, transmission, transformation, and utilization of information. This includes the investigation of information representations in both natural and artificial systems, the use of codes for efficient message transmission, and the study of information processing devices and techniques such as computers and their programming systems. It is an interdisciplinary science derived from and related to such fields as mathematics, logic, linguistics, psychology, computer technology, operations research, the graphic arts, communications, library science, management, and other similar fields. It has both a pure science component, which inquires into the subject without regard to its application, and an applied science component, which develops services and products.

If this definition seems complicated, it is because the subject matter is complex and multidimensional, and the definition is intended to be all-encompassing.

Obviously information science is not the exclusive domain of any one organization. Traditionally, the American Documentation Institute has been concerned with the study of recorded, that is, documentary, information. This is still our main emphasis; however, the work is now embedded in a larger context. Librarianship and documentation are applied aspects of information science. The techniques and procedures used by librarians and documentalists are, or should be, based upon the theoretical findings of information science, and conversely the theoretician should study the time-tested techniques of the practitioner.

## The Need for Information Science

Information science as a discipline has as its goal to provide a body of information that will lead to improvements in the various institutions and procedures dedicated to the accumulation and transmission of knowledge. There are in existence a number of such institutions and related media: These include *books* for packaging knowledge; *schools* for teaching the accumulated knowledge of many generations; *libraries* for storing and disseminating knowledge; *movies* and television for the visual display of knowledge; *journals* for the written communication of the latest technical advances in specialized fields; and *conferences* for the oral communication of information.

These institutions have served, and continue to serve, very useful functions, but they are inadequate to meet the communication needs of today's society. Some of the factors that contribute to their inadequacies are:

1. The tremendous growth in science and technology and the accelerated pace at which new knowledge becomes available and old knowledge becomes obsolete;

2. The fast rate of obsolescence of technical knowledge, so that the old graduate must go back to school and update his skills;

3. The large number of working scientists and the large number of scientific and technical journals which exist today;

4. The increased specialization which makes communication and the exchange of information between disciplines very difficult;

5. The short time lag between research and application that makes the need for information more pressing, and more immediate.

As a result of these pressures, the existing methods for exchanging information have been found wanting. Information science has not kept pace with other scientific developments, and now there is a need to concentrate efforts in this field and to catch up. If communication and information exchange procedures are not improved, all other scientific work will be impeded; the lack of communication will result in a duplication of effort and a slowing of progress.

The importance of information science and the reasons for the current emphasis upon this discipline are thus clear: The need to organize our efforts and meet the new challenges finds a concrete expression in the American Society for Information Science.

## Information Science Research and Applications

As was pointed out in the definition, information science has both a pure and an applied aspect. Members of this discipline, depending upon their training and interests, will emphasize one or the other aspect. Within information science there is room for both the theoretician and the practitioner, and clearly both are needed. Theory and practice are inexorably related; each feeds on the work of the other.

The researcher in information science has a broad field in which to pursue his investigations. A glance through the 566 pages (excluding the Glossary and Index) of the last issue (No. 14) of *Current Research and Development in Scientific Documentation* (2) shows a staggering range of projects being studied. The 655 project statements are organized into nine categories as follows:

1. *Information Needs and Uses*
   Behavioral studies of users; citation studies; communication patterns; literature use studies.

2. *Document Creation and Copying*
   Computer-assisted composition; microforms; recording and storing; writing and editing.

3. *Language Analysis*
   Computational linguistics; lexicography; natural language (text) processing; psycholinguistics; semantic analysis.

4. *Translation*
   Machine translation; translation aids.

5. *Abstracting, Classification, Coding and Indexing*
   Classification and indexing systems; content analysis; machine-aided classification, extracting and indexing; vocabulary studies.

6. *System Design*
   Information centers; information retrieval; mechanization of library operations; selective dissemination of information.

7. *Analysis and Evaluation*
   Comparative studies; indexing quality; modeling; test methods and performance measures; translation quality.

8. *Pattern Recognition*
   Image processing; speech analysis.

9. *Adaptive Systems*
   Artificial intelligence; automata; problem solving; self-organizing systems.

In essence, information science research investigates the properties and behavior of information, the use and transmission of information, and the processing of information for optimal storage and retrieval.

Theoretic studies should not, and in fact do not, take place in a vacuum. There is a constant interplay between research and application, between theory and practice. As in most every scientifically based discipline, the researchers form a small but vocal minority. The bulk of the membership is applications oriented. These members deal, on a daily basis, with the problems and practices of information transfer. They are responsible for making the system work in spite of all inadequacies, and they develop improvements within an operational context. They need to be informed about the new techniques being developed and when these are proven, they need to apply them and evaluate them under operating conditions. Yet, it is important to recognize that, particularly in information science, there is no sharp distinction between research and technology. It is a matter of emphasis, and all members share a concern over a common set of problems.

Every scientific discipline needs an academic component, and so it is important to note that information science is now a recognized discipline in an increasing number of major universities. The subjects taught vary from school to school, probably more as a function of available professorial skills rather than any real difference of opinion about what should be taught. Such diversity is desirable. The field is too young, and it is too soon to standardize on a single curriculum, for a variety of programs encourages exploration and growth. As students graduate, they will exert a unifying and maturing influence on the educational program.

## Summary

By way of a summary, I will restate the questions and answers that led to this essay on information science. Again, I would like to add the caveat that these are not meant to be final answers but rather to serve as foci for further discussion and clarification.

*What is information science?* It is an interdisciplinary science that investigates the properties and behavior of information, the forces that govern the flow and use of information, and the techniques, both manual and mechanical, of processing information for optimal storage, retrieval, and dissemination.

*What then is documentation?* Documentation is one of many applied components of information science. Documentation is concerned with acquiring, storing, retrieving, and disseminating recorded documentary information, primarily in the form of report and journal literature. Because of the nature of the collection and the user's requirements, documentation has tended to emphasize the use of data processing equipment, reprography and microforms as techniques of information handling.

*What does an information scientist do?* Information scientists may work as researchers, educators, or applications specialists in the field of information science; that is to say, they may do research aimed at developing new techniques of information handling; they may teach information science; and they may apply the theories and techniques of information science to create, modify and improve information handling systems.

Information science is an important emergent discipline, and the information scientist has an important function in our society.

## Postscript

This article was written and submitted to the Editor of American Documentation in September 1967. Clearly the members of ASIS are not the only people worried about the vocabulary of information science and technology, for in October 1967, Mr. Samuel A. Miles, a member of the Society of Technical Writers and Editors and also a member of ASIS, published a paper entitled "An Introduction to the Vocabulary of Information Technology" in

*Technical Communications*, the journal for STWP. The general purpose of this paper was to familiarize the technical writer with the activities and the vocabulary of the information processor. To do this, Mr. Miles selected ten basic terms and their definitions from the proposed ASA standards and from the DoD glossary. These terms are similar to and supplement the terms in the Information Science article.

In this ecumenical atmosphere, it is good to know that other societies are equally concerned with the workings of information science, and it is a pleasant duty to reference the work of Mr. Samuel A. Miles.*

## References

1. Taylor, R. S., Professional Aspects of Information Science and Technology, in C. A. Cuadra (Ed.), *Annual Review of Information Science and Technology,* Vol. 1, John Wiley & Sons, New York, 1966.

2. NATIONAL SCIENCE FOUNDATION, *Current Research and Development in Scientific Documentation,* No. 14, Office of Scientific Information, NSF-66-17,Washington, D.C., 1966.

---

*Miles, Samuel A., An Introduction to the Vocabulary of Information Technology, Technical Communications, Fall Quarter 1967, pp. 20–24.

---

## Opinion Paper

# Towards a Metascience of Information: Informatology

### Klause Otten and Anthony DeBons*

Reprinted with permission of John Wiley & Sons, Inc.: Published in the *Journal of the American Society for Information Science,* January–February 1970, pp. 89–94.

Arguments are advanced to suggest that information and operations on information are phenomena, the principles of which provide the basis for a metascience of information (informatology). The fundamental character of the phenomena is evidenced in the operations executed during the processing and communication functions. The role of the metascience is dictated by

---

*Respectively, The National Cash Register Company, Dayton, Ohio, and Dept. of Information Science, University of Dayton, Dayton, Ohio.

several factors, namely, the need for a common basis upon which all information-oriented specialized sciences and technologies can be understood and studied, a common framework and language for all scientists and technologists concerned in some form or other with information, and the need to integrate various theories that concern themselves with the phenomena of information on one side and man's relationship to the phenomena on the other side. The content of the postulated metascience of information is circumscribed by a list of specific questions and problems for which the science has to provide answers and solutions. It is suggested that an educational concept responsive to the needs of metascience of information be developed and implemented.

## Introduction

The emergence of a new discipline concerned with theories on information has been proposed by Gorn *(1)* and others. The importance of the new discipline for all sectors of human activities and development, especially in education, has been discussed. In this paper, an attempt is made to outline the nature and content of this new discipline in the hope that it might provide the basis for further examination and discussion.

Information, both as a commodity and as a basic phenomenon is gaining importance in all activities of man. We seek information, we exchange information, we "use" information, in many contexts. We have developed entire technologies centered around information and its dissemination, e.g., the arts of recording (writing and printing), of broadcasting (advertising, publishing, radio and TV broadcasting), of transmitting (postal systems, telephone and telegraph, satellite communications), and of processing information (computers), to name just the more important ones. As a phenomenon in its own right, we have been made aware of the pervasion of information and operations on information through nature and human society, in the communication between cells of any organism, in the information exchange between living creatures and within social systems.

To explore the nature of information and operations thereupon as phenomena, two questions have to be raised: (1) Does information represent a fundamental and universal phenomenon similar to matter and energy? (2) Are the various operations performed on information based on fundamental phenomena and are they hence only different forms of some fundamental relations?

If the answers to the above two questions are essentially affirmative, then we believe that the body of knowledge describing these phenomena and relations will evolve as the subject of a new science. This proposed new science, by its nature of unifying concepts now included as part of established sciences and by the postulated need to derive formalistic descriptions, may be referred to as a metascience *(2)*. More specifically, it may be referred to as a metascience of information.

To expand on this concept we have established several objectives for this paper. The first objective is to show that the answers to the two questions raised appear to be affirmative and that a metascience of information is emerging. The second objective is to outline the basis for the development of a metascience of information. The third objective is to state the specific goals of such a metascience and distinguish these objectives from those of existing related sciences.

## Information and Operations on Information as Fundamental Phenomena

### Basic Constituents of Information

First, we want to distinguish between information and operations on information. Information, like energy, can be viewed as a fundamental phenomenon. Energy is manifested in a variety of attributes (heat, electrical energy, chemical energy, etc.). Similarly, the attributes of information are experienced in various forms (knowledge, news, etc.). Energy can be described abstractly and analytically independent of its form. Likewise one might postulate that information can be approached on the same terms.

Operations on information, on the other side can be compared to the various forms by which energy can be manipulated, e.g., the conversion of heat into electricity, chemical energy into heat, etc. These manipulations on energy obey certain fundamental laws. In the same way one can postulate that operations on information will obey its own set of fundamental laws.

The various phenomena to which we refer to as "information" (i.e., human communications, computations, automated control) contain invariant components irrespective of the particular form (news, knowledge, etc.). Likewise the multitude of operations that can be performed on these phenomena appear to be composed of invariant components. It is therefore logical to pursue the development of formalistic and abstract descriptions of these invariant components as we will describe later.

All information processing operations can be performed by digital computers. To achieve this general information processing by computers, the processes have to be decomposed into a number of elementary operations. It is this set of elementary operations that constitutes the building blocks for all complex information processing in nature or machinery.

This recognition of the fundamental nature of information processing has evolved slowly. Information processing in the past has been the privilege of man. "White collar" professions, that is, professions centered around information processing activities, developed. Information processing in these professions ranges from routine clerical chores to the demanding intellectual activities of a diagnostician, researcher, or manager. The variety of information processing activities, and hence of white collar professions, increases rapidly.

Along with the diversification of information processing tasks goes a gradual takeover of information processing by machines. First, machines were invented to perform elementary calculations; that is, fundamental information processes on numbers only. It was later found that the same types of machines could handle many nonnumerical repetitive chores usually handled by clerks. Gradually computers have entered all areas of information processing. They execute a wide variety of complex operations on information that conventionally had been performed by man in the fields of business, industry, research, education, and in other areas. These complex operations are not performed by specialized machines but by computers, which can perform only a limited number of elementary logic operations.

How is it possible that many of our operations on information, such as comparing, calculating, extrapolating, analyzing, and even reading, writing, composing, and designing can be performed by one and the same machine, executing only elementary operations? We must assume that the apparently different information processing tasks all have some common basis. *This common basis must be expressable in terms of the elementary operations executed by the computer. The ability to translate complex information processing tasks into sequences of elementary operations may be accepted as evidence for the fundamental nature of information and of information processing.*

The fundamental nature of information per se can also be demonstrated by the processes of information transmission or communications in general. Any transmission link can, in principle, be used to transmit every kind of information. A communication channel provides the means for the transmission of information. This involves the transmission of a physical signal. However, this signal can be used to convey any form of information. For example, it can convey information expressed in the language of computers, information in the form of speech, of graphics, or even of motion pictures (TV). The operations performed in transmitting the various physical representations of information are one and the same; that is, the engineer can design his communication system without knowing the nature of information being transmitted as long as he knows the quality of information being transmitted. In brief: the fundamental character of information and of information processing is suggested by the nature of several operations on information. It is primarily indicated by the facts that:

1. All different forms of information processing can be performed by serial execution of a few elementary operations (computers used for simulation), and

2. Information in all of its different forms is transmittable by one and the same process (communications).

## Theories Underlining the Fundamental Nature of Information and of Operations on Information

Indications of the commonality of information phenomena have, of course, been well studied from various points of view. As a result, we have a number of theories attempting either to describe selected information phenomena in a quantitative form or to establish a common basis for the study of information phenomena in two or more related fields.

Information theory is the outgrowth of an attempt to measure whatever can be transmitted over a communication channel of given measurable physical properties. Information in information theory is a probabilistic quantity, a measure of an expectation value: The probability of occurrence of an event prior to its observation. Information is viewed as the result of stochastic selection process (from a defined set of alternatives); hence, the measurable quantity is named "selective" information. Consequently, information-theory deals with one specific aspect and type of information. It does not deal with many other (particularly semantic) forms that we generally refer to as information. Most important, it does not provide a theory for "information" as used and valued by man in his daily actions.

The common concept of information is qualitative and can be distinguished from the selective information concept as that of semantic information. Ultimately, semantic information would have to be measured in terms of the conceptual system of the user; man. Linguists and semanticists are in search of a measure for semantic information but have not as yet succeeded in finding one.

Various other mathematical theories have received impetus from the rapidly developing information technologies and have resulted in the branching off of specialized information-oriented disciplines of mathematics. Examples are coding theory (evolving from set and function theories in response to needs in the field of communication), and the theory of finite automata (evolving from the theories of computability in response to needs of designers of algorithmic programs, in particular, of programs simulating human recognition functions).

Other examples can be derived from the various system theories. Theories describing the behavior of dynamic systems have evolved in response to the need for full control over the design of electric signal processing systems. These theories serve as the link between physical characteristics of system components and system responses to signals. Since signals are carriers of information, any form of signal processing is an operation on information. Theories of dynamic systems initially were derived to account for relations between electrical signals and structures of electrical components, often referred to as systems. Consequently, theories of dynamic systems have been recognized as theories describing the behavior of any signal in any systems that are analogous to electrical systems.

All of these theories given as examples attempt to describe the invariance of information and hence can be considered as building blocks of the metascience of information.

# The Development of a Science of Information

### The Concept of Metascience and
### the Functions of a Metascience

Human desires and needs lead to the development of technologies: The advancement of these technologies requires explanations to technological questions that arise. Hence, the advancing technologies stimulate research and lead to the development of sciences. As the technologies progress, research and, correspondingly, the resulting sciences become more and more specialized. More and more sciences evolve, sciences that become narrower and narrower in specialization. As a result, the chances for fertile and productive communication between related specialized sciences decrease.

In response to trends of higher and higher specialization, usually, a counteraction takes place; the need for communication between sciences leads to a re-evaluation of the foundations of related specialized sciences.

These re-evaluations stimulate the formulation of new simplifying and unifying theories that subsume the main concepts of the original theories of contributing sciences. These unified theories may be considered as the body of a new science, which may be named the metascience for those sciences for which the metascience provides the unifying foundation.[1]

Metasciences provide the common language and the means for translating concepts among divergent fields and as such, assist in unification of knowledge in general. Metasciences serve three important functions:

1. They permit the description of the common basis of related disciplines at a higher level of abstraction than possible within the framework of the individual contributing disciplines.

2. They provide a common language for scientists and technologists in divergent fields of specialization.

3. They establish the means for translating knowledge gained in one field to other related fields.

Metasciences require precise and abstract formalizations and definitions of the foundations of all related sciences, thereby strengthening the foundations

---

[1]The evolution of formal mathematics (which is referred to as metamathematics) is an example of this type of science evolution. Metamathematics provides the unified foundation of all specialized disciplines of mathematics.

of the sciences under unification through the metascience. Evolving meta-sciences stimulate the advancement of the specialized sciences and contribute to the knowledge transfer between otherwise isolated disciplines.

The specialization of sciences in our century has led to the evolution of several metasciences in the sense of unifying base sciences, even though they are usually not identified as such. We have already referred to the metascience of mathematics: "formal mathematics." As another example, we may cite the parallel developments of theories used for the analysis and synthesis in the fields of mechanical systems, acoustical systems, and electrical. For each of these systems, specialized theories evolved. However, the analogies between phenomena observed in these three disciplines lead to the development of the general theories of linear and nonlinear dynamic systems. These theories are equally applicable to any one of the three types of systems as well as to other physical systems. These general system theories can be considered as the "Metatheories" for the various fields of dynamic system technologies.

Other illustrations of metasciences can be obtained from linguistics, which can be regarded as the metascience for the body of knowledge on languages and their use for communication.

As metamathematics evolved in response to the divergence and growths of specialized mathematical disciplines, similarly, we anticipate the evolution of a metascience of information in response to the need for a critical reevaluation of the foundation upon which many information disciplines and technologies are based. This anticipated metascience can be viewed as the science of information (or informatology). Informatology can be defined as the study of the fundamental principles underlying the structure and use of information.

## The Metascience of Information

Sciences and technologies centered around the phenomena of information are mushrooming. Diverging disciplines of ever increasing specialization grow in response to the "information explosion." For that reason, the need for a unifying science appears apparent.

Need for the existence of the metascience of information can be demonstrated by the following factors:

1. There is a need to provide a common basis upon which all information-oriented specialized sciences and technologies can be understood and studied.

2. A common framework and language must be established to serve technologists concerned with information in some form or other.

3. There is the need to build bridges between the abstract theories attempting theoretical explanations of the phenomena of information on the one

side and between the (at present predominately empirical) theories describing man's relationship to information phenomena on the other side.

Information is generated, processed, and used by men. If machines are involved in handling information, these machines generate, process and use information under the control by man and for man. Thus, the metascience of information has two focal points: the phenomena of information and man's relation to the phenomena.

Man sets the limit to what can be done with information. As ultimate user and, in many cases, as generator of information, his information processing capabilities determine the usefulness of information systems to him individually or collectively. This statement concerning man as the point of reference applies even to the functions of hypothesized supermachines exhibiting artificial intelligence exceeding that of exceptional human performance.

It must be recognized however, that the complexity of man's relation to information and of his information processing, prevent man, at this time, from being the test bed for information sciences. The theories forming the body for the metascience of information may have to evolve slowly. They have to be based on elementary information relations that can be examined and verified under controlled conditions in man-made form and environment. The application of these fundamental laws and relations in more and more complex systems ultimately have to be applicable to man and always have to serve man.

The ultimate orientation of a metascience of information toward man as the user of information does not exclude the development of information processes for which neither nature nor man provide examples. The evolution of artificial intelligence in the sense of intellectual or information generating power exceeding that of man is conceivable. Yet, it always has to be under the control and submission to man as its originator and user.

## Questions to Be Answered by Metascience of Information

The objectives and the content of the postulated metascience of information may become more evident if we look at the major questions for which it has to provide answers.

1. Can the concept of selective information be extended to permit the measurement of semantic or qualitative information? If so, how; if not, what concept of semantic or qualitative information allows quantitative analysis? (Information Theory, Semantics)[2]

---

[2]Specific disciplines are quoted in parentheses, which are concerned with the specific area.

2. Can the various forms of information processing be analyzed in the form of common elementary processes and can these processes be described by fundamental laws? (Mathematical Logic, Automata Theory, Computer Sciences)

3. How can different methods of information processings, which achieve the same results, be compared, and what are suitable quantitative measures that will enable the differentiation of the complexity and efficiency of operations on information? (Computer Sciences, Computational Linguistics)

4. How does man associate meaning with information, and what is the relationship between meaning and his established value system? (Psychology, Philosophy, Semantics)

5. What are the laws that make natural languages[3] the universal means of formulating (creating) and communicating new concepts and ideas? (Linguistics, Semantics)

   Natural languages in the widest sense (including music and forms of artistic expression) permit the creation of new concepts. Even if there exists no equivalent (in nature or in man's history) for these new concepts, they become immediately understandable to persons other than the creator by virtue of the context of the language and the situation. Are there fundamental laws that govern the conditions under which "creation" can take place and how can new creations (concepts) be understood if the description can only indirectly suggest a thought process?

6. What are the interrelations between the forms of energy, matter, and order (or structure), and the use of these forms to represent (selective) information?

   Selective information, when communicated, is always associated with some form of physical representation: as matter, or energy, or both (molecules in genetic code; energy quanta in communications via light). The degree of order of the physical form is correlated with information. What are the laws that govern the ordered use of matter or energy to represent information?

7. What are the physical limitations of communication, information processing, and information storage? (Communication Theory, Brain Research, Research in Memory Technology)

---

[3]Natural languages are codes of communication resulting from an evolutionary process of culture. In the narrow sense these are spoken languages, e.g., English, French, etc., in the wide sense they include, e.g., music and art.

Neither energy nor matter are continua. The smallest units of energy (quanta) and matter (atoms, nuclear particles) set absolute lower bounds to the information that can be represented by given physical systems or processes.

8. What are the laws governing the organization of information as it applies to mass information storage and retrieval? (Experimental Psychology, Library Sciences, Computer Science, Brain Research)

9. What are the laws of information dissemination which explain the processes of cognitive perception? (Educational Psychology, Theories of Self-Adaptive Systems, Cybernetics)

10. Are there properties of information which stimulate creativity and is creativity an information processing function for which laws can be developed? (Cybernetics, Artificial Intelligence, Semantics)

11. What are the laws of information accumulation, updating, and assimilation? (Educational Psychology, Library Sciences, Computer Sciences)

The foregoing problem areas do not exhaust all the possible questions that are the domain of a metascience of information. They are suggestive of the nature of the questions and, as such, should serve to circumscribe the anticipated content of the science.

## Metascience of Information and Its Relation to Other Sciences

Metascience of information, as indirectly defined by the major questions for which it has to provide answers, is a science by itself. However, it has concerns common with other sciences and disciplines. This is schematically shown in Fig. 1 [see Figure 2.1]. As a metascience, it shares with the related sciences the formalistic descriptions of the respective science foundations. If this were the full content of the science, it would not require separate identity. However, the metascience's main contribution is the function it plays in synthesizing the various formalistic descriptions into one unified set of theories which is equally applicable to all contributor sciences and disciplines. There are numerous new disciplines concerned directly with some selected phenomena of information. We have to investigate the differences between some of those sciences and our postulated metascience to show that none of the following sciences by itself is aimed at answering all of the questions listed above.

Computer sciences are concerned with the processing of information, particularly by digital computers. Emphasis is on the analysis and synthesis of information processing operations and on the implementation of those by computers. Questions concerning the communication of information and the use of information by man are of secondary importance. The focal points are algorithmic processing and computer technology. Computer sciences are concerned principally with information and information processes as is the metascience of information. However, the information-oriented problems in computer sciences are centered around computers as processor and are hence specialized. The metascience of information, in contrast, is studying and describing the fundamental concepts of information and operation on information regardless of its main function—its theories must be equally applicable to computers, biological systems, man, social systems and man-made information systems.

A comparison of the metascience of information with cybernetics is difficult, since cybernetics has different meanings to different people. Let us refer to cybernetics by Wiener *(3)* ("Cybernetics as science of control and communication in the animal and machine.") Cybernetics, according to this definition, is centered around control and communication: control of systems to achieve desired objectives, and communication of information to support the control functions. The focal point for cybernetics is control. Information in its various forms is essential to the cybernetician, but always as the means to exercise or achieve control. In contrast, the postulated metascience has information, per se, not its use, as its focal point. The particular use of information and information processing is of secondary interest. Cybernetics can perhaps be viewed as the metascience of purposeful dynamic systems in general.

Finally, we have to comment on the various forms of "information science" ranging from the narrowly defined library and documentation science concepts to the all-inclusive claims for an information science. Information science, in the sense of documentation and library science, is oriented toward one sector of the postulated metascience: the laws of classification and of mass information storage and retrieval. To date, this library-oriented information science has been preoccupied with developing improvements of documented message handling and has not been able to devote much effort toward the study of the laws underlying these operations. Therefore, information science in the library science sense represents primarily a technology, with some science-oriented aspects that can be considered as sub-fields of the postulated metascience.

Definitions of information science have been suggested that are all inclusive: as sciences concerned with all aspects of information. Our definition of metascience of information should clearly not be misunderstood as one of an all inclusive science. We view the metascience of information as a very specific science, concerned only with the foundations of information-related sciences and technologies and not concerned with the content of these specialized disciplines. Any claim for all-inclusiveness would lead to superficiality and therefore would not serve any purpose.

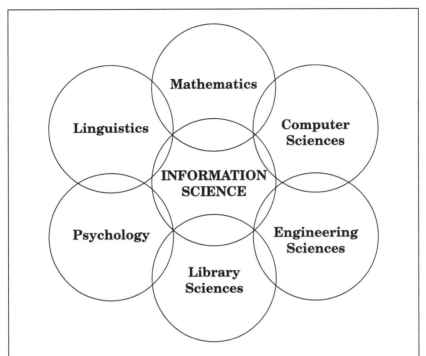

**Figure 2.1** Information Science and Related Sciences. (Schematic two dimensional representation of an n-dimensional relationship—only the most important related sciences are shown.)

## Training Requirements for a Metascience of Information

Based on the foregoing, we will argue that the training for future information scientists should be started now by the development of an integrated information science curriculum in which information science is understood as the evolving metascience of information.

The metascience of information requires a special training for its successful development. Information scientists, in contrast to information technologists, need to be oriented toward the objectives of integrating present and future knowledge of the laws inherent in information phenomena. They require carefully developed inter-disciplinary skills. Tools and concepts from engineering, computer science, library science, and psychology should be coupled with an understanding of fundamental sciences such as mathematics. In this way, students can apply their understanding to the formulation of meaningful research, which may help in establishing the laws and theories for the metascience discussed in this paper.

## Acknowledgments

Appreciation is expressed to Dr. Carlos Crocetti, Rome Air Development Center, Rome, N.Y., and to Dr. Vladimir Slamecka, of the Georgia Institute of Technology, for their helpful comments and suggestions.

## References

1. Saul Gorn, The Computer and Information Sciences and the Community of Disciplines, *Behavioral Sciences,* 12:433–452 (1967).

2. Stephen, C. Keene, *Introduction to Metamathematics,* D. Van Nostrand Co., Inc., Princeton, NJ., 1950.

3. Norbert, Wiener, *Cybernetics,* The M.I.T. Press, Cambridge, Mass. 1948, 1961.

# Chapter 3

# Communication

## Introduction

One of the frequent confusions about information's identity is that it is communication. While information and communication are intricately connected and have some aspects that seem similar, they are not the same. Communication involves process, or the movement of information, or potential information. Information and communication are impacted by context. Context may provide dimensions to information or to communication; these dimensions influence the outcome of the communication or the interpretation of the information. Technical aspects of communication compared to human communication, such as the signal quality versus the content and interpretation of the signal, are context dependent. One of the more influential theories of communication originated with a question about an electronic signal transmission. Modifying that theory to be more applicable to the human communication and information models provides insight into the special issues of information and human communication.

## Communication and Information

In the context of an electronic signal, communication is the process whereby a signal is transmitted from a source via some channel to a recipient. The signal is sent from a beginning point through a channel, such as a wire or cable, to a receiver. For example, an electrical signal, generated by dialing a phone number, is carried over phone wires to the appropriate telephone set where the signal is received (Schramm, 1973). This perspective on communication is credited to Norbert Wiener's book *Cybernetics*, and Claude Shannon's paper "The Mathematical Theory of Communication" (Young, 1987). It was in the context of an electronics and engineering problem for which Shannon proposed the mathematical theory of communication, a theory to measure the amount of information in a signal. His theory revolved around a statistical formula to determine the amount of deviation from a code the signal could tolerate and be received in a state that could be decoded. Shannon's interest was in the quality of the transmission, not in the meaning of the signal (Ritchie, 1991; Schramm; Young). Noise in the channel, such as static, could interfere with the clarity of a signal such that the receiver would have difficulty distinguishing the intended signal from other signals. Such difficulty would contribute to uncertainty, that is, make it difficult to decode the signal correctly. Uncertainty in this context meant that the receiver had to select among various possibilities to determine the correct signal. Shannon opposed the application of his theory to other than its specific problem (Bar-Hillel, 1964; Ritchie), though it was his coauthor Warren Weaver (1949) of the book *The Mathematical Theory of Communication*, who suggested it could be applied to other areas of communication (Ritchie; Serverin and Tankard, 1992). There continues to be controversy about the appropriateness of the extension of Shannon's theory outside of the specific domain of its original development. Nonetheless, this theory has been the basis of many new interpretations of activities in a variety of disciplines (Shera, 1983; Tribus, 1983; Young).

In a generalized context, the concepts underlying the theory may be extended to a broader vision of communication. Communication involves the sending of a signal of some type through some medium to a receiver (Schramm, 1973). When a cat cries, the sound itself is a signal, the sound is carried through the air, the channel, and received by your eardrums, which the sound causes to vibrate. When you speak, your voice is a signal carried by the air to the ears of whomever is present; they are the receivers. However, if you stand perfectly still, saying nothing, you are still communicating, sending a signal, via a different medium (visual rather than audible). The signal may be construed as information. As mentioned earlier, information is a concept that is difficult to define and we subscribe to the notion that there is nothing that is not information. In this framework, communication then is a process involving transmission of information, in whatever form via whatever vehicle, to a receiver, or decoder. Information is a component in the process of communication. Information may be the core of the activity, as in trying to distribute research information, it may be incidental to the process, as in "small talk." Communication may be the result of processing information, or the cause of processing it, as when someone tells you a riddle and you attempt to process the information into a solution. Schramm states that "information is the stuff of communication. It is what distinguishes communication from, say swimming or bouncing a ball... (p. 38)." Schramm views communication as an activity essential to the organization of human society, culture, relationships, and survival. The movement, exchange, and processing of information are the underlying, and possibly unconscious, impetus to engage in acts of communication. Such acts are part of building a community, defining a standard of conduct, establishing an identity within a group, or even being in touch with one's self.

How is it that the movement of information is so involved with humanity and seems so important? Information may describe, characterize, or model the world. The color of the sky informs us of aspects of the weather—a clear blue sky tells us of a different sort of weather than a gray-black cloudy sky. Experience helps us to identify which of these colors indicates good weather or bad weather. How is that information shared without the experience? It is done by the communication of others who relay this measure of weather to us, as we compare their information to our experience at a later time. The shape of a mountain may convey information about its formation, just as the color of a gem or mineral indicates its origins in the earth. The information may reside in the object, it may be inferred, it may be communicated by human exchange or merely by human observation and interpretation. Schramm (1973) makes the point that information and communication are not limited to languages, or words. There are verbal and nonverbal communications that transmit information, and they may be culturally specific. Information may be communicated not necessarily by what is said, but by the fact that someone finds it important enough to say. Information may also be gleaned from how it is communicated, such as choice of words, level of excitement, tone of voice, speed of speech, the pitch of music, or even movements and moments of silence. Communication involves a transmission—a sending of something, not necessarily words, or electronic tones; it may be images, physical signals such as hand or flag waving; it may be sound, or not—but it has a source and a recipient.

## Information, Uncertainty, and Communication

Information has been defined in many ways, including the grand explanation in the first chapter, but it is necessary to clarify how the word and its adjuncts will be considered here in context with communication (Dervin and Nilan, 1986). Information is input from any source that has the potential to affect, reduce, or supplement a state of uncertainty to allow decisions to be made or communication to occur. Uncertainty has many circumstantial definitions, but in the context with which we are concerned, it can be construed as the probable amount of information available. The greater the uncertainty, the less information is available.

Decreasing uncertainty requires gaining more information, but increasing information may not always resolve uncertainty. Uncertainty may be the measure of how many alternatives are available and the possibility of their outcome. When deciding which road to follow at a complex intersection, the amount of uncertainty is related to the number of roads at the intersection and how much other information is available about the roads. The uncertainty could be reduced if there were a sign on any one of the roads that indicated whether it was a north–south or east–west road, or if a sign indicating miles to a specific town were available.

Adding information to the situation decreases the uncertainty and improves the decision process. If you see a bird and think that it is a bluebird, but are not certain, the method to solve the question is to consult a birding book. What if upon checking the book you find that the bird is indeed not a bluebird, but you have no idea what type of bird it is? The information that solved whether it was a bluebird or not did not provide the answer to the real question, what type of bird is it? You have decreased uncertainty by ruling out one type of bird, but overall you have not resolved the problem. In the case of the bird, if you continue to look at pictures and ask bird experts, you are likely to resolve the problem and reduce uncertainty to zero. At some point you will be able to determine without a doubt the identity of the bird by selecting alternatives and accepting or ruling them out.

There are many situations, especially in science, management, and finance where it is not possible to reduce uncertainty as completely. For example, when selecting a stock, you may perform extensive research to evaluate a given company's historical stock performance, the behavior of the management team, and the current and predicted status of the market in which they operate. You could even statistically analyze the last thirty years of stock prices, but you will not be able to eliminate all uncertainty. Possession of all this information will not ensure that the stock goes up, as you cannot be in possession of all the information that influences the stock market. You will not be able to eliminate all the possible alternatives or their outcomes. Some of the reasons for that uncertainty have to do with communication. The movement and availability of information to resolve all the uncertainty in such a complex system are currently beyond our capacity to control. Information and communication have a complex relationship, but they are not the same. Communication moves information, information may reduce uncertainty, communication has a relationship to uncertainty via information. But, communication may even contribute to uncertainty. The actors in the communication system may influence how information is transmitted, by what channels, and how it is received. What if it were suggested that one of your favorite stocks is about to crash? How you received the information, who sent it, and how sensitive you are that day to such a threat will influence how you respond to the information, that is, whether you accept it, or reject it.

## *Passive or Active, It Is Communication*

Information exposure may be passive, that is, the potential recipient or user is exposed but does not necessarily pursue or consciously apply the information. An example would be television commercials that were seen but not consciously noted, yet did influence a shopping choice via recognition of a product name. An act of communication did occur: the television was the sender, your unconscious mind, the receiver. Indirect application of information would be unintentional retention of information in memory and use of this unrecognized information in resolution activities. Or, information exposure may be active, where the information is pursued and/or applied consciously. In this case, the television commercial caused the recipient of the information to look for a specific product or consciously seek to purchase such a product. Again, an act of communication occurred, and it had a conscious effect.

Direct application of information is intentional storage in memory or acknowledgement of information received. When information is stored in memory, an act of communication has occurred from the external world to the mind's internal world. Another direct application would be the use of the information to cope with a specific problem, decision, or uncertainty reduction process. Information pursuit, or use, is actively attempting to obtain some value from information. Information seeking is a process involving a behavioral activity, or a set of activities, to obtain information believed to be necessary to affect a state of uncertainty or to evoke a communication. Each of the above information-related notions are entwined with communication. Acts of communication may be directed actions undertaken to gain information to decrease uncertainty, or may be almost passive acts where information is transmitted and received without overt effort on the part of the recipient.

## Channels

The medium by which information is transmitted is the channel. A person carrying messages may be a channel; a radio or a billboard may be a channel. There are also information roles in the communication act: the person carrying the messages is an information transmitter if all he/she does is carry the message. However, if the messenger also located and collected the information he/she might be an information provider, an economic context of the communication act and the information dynamic. The radio, however, is a technological channel. The radio announcers may be channels, or information providers, or information producers or information seekers attempting to gather information for application, but they are actors in a communication exchange.

Two hundred years ago the stagecoach was an information channel, indeed, a part of a communication system. The riders carried newspapers, letters, and information collected on the ride, the state of the passage. They also carried the news of the places from which they traveled, from the people with whom they had spoken. Strangers traveling in this country years ago would be invited to stop to visit, as they were sources of information about places they had been, or people they may have encountered, or just the gossip of the time. As much of the knowledge of the West was not written, Indian scouts and wagon train masters who had traveled the West and were familiar with the special difficulties of an area were accorded a certain respect for the information they possessed. There was more faith in a person than in the words of a book that many could not read and few trusted with their lives. Access to information was limited by time and distance. Later, the wireless was a monumental new channel for carrying information, but word of mouth and long delayed letters were maintained into the twentieth century as potent information sources.

Modern channels such as the telephone, television, radio, computer networks, telecommunications, fax machines, and daily newspapers allow us to obtain information much faster than in the days of the stagecoach. More than speed, however, these new channels opened other doors and changed our society. Just as industrialization changed the work roles and social structures of this country, so too have changes in the technology of communication and information affected our lives. Instead of Pony Express mail carriers, we can fax materials to be received within minutes of transmission. Instead of waiting for European newspapers to arrive in ports and travel across country, we can see the news in virtually any corner of the globe by turning on the television or accessing the Web. The Indian scouts and wagon masters have been replaced with maps, available in the supermarket next to the guidebook of interesting sights. The maps replaced one aspect of their knowledge, but not their stories and insights missed by the map, or what physical information they brought. Maps do not have the accumulated experience that allowed the scouts and wagon masters to survive the unexpected, to make choices to preserve their charges. A person armed with a map can follow a route but does not have the added resource of the experienced guide who can make decisions when the weather goes foul or the map is out of date. The map is a communication medium, but its information content is dependent upon the user's ability to extract information from the object. Possession of information yields power when only a select few could read a map, which imbued them with power. The increased availability of maps and their potential information create an illusion that anyone can access the information. In theory this is true, but in fact, using the information requires prior knowledge, which is not automatically available by mere possession of the map.

Much of what was carried in the oral traditions is now printed material or even visual media. We read to our children the stories from books, we watch re-enactments of life on video. A stranger is not considered a potential message carrier and is not invited to visit without a great deal of unease. Our society tends to believe the printed word over the spoken word; contracts are drawn to protect us so that we can debate them in court. Some communications have been formalized into special situations that tend to cause them to be perceived as more valid, such as statements in a court of law, the communication between doctor and patient, or religious guide and supplicant. Where once we relied upon and trusted only the human communication system, we now substitute artifacts in print and other media.

## Human Experience, Information, and Communication

Schramm (1973) characterizes communication as a manner of extending one's senses and improving one's ability to interact with the surrounding world. Schramm expanded upon Shannon's theory of information and communication to overcome the limitations of the basic model provided by the sender-channel-receiver pattern. Invoking human qualities, Schramm includes human experience as part of the system of both the sender and receiver in human communication. Further, Schramm, unlike Shannon, was interested in the meaning of the signal sent through the channel. Schramm suggests that human experience contributes to channel "noise," this and the added feature of feedback together impact the transmission and decoding of signals (Severin and Tankard, 1992). If one has never seen or heard of an elephant, it might be difficult to comprehend the size or appearance of the creature. Few of us have ever walked on the moon; most of us can only imagine the way the moon-ground feels beneath the foot, or how it feels to lumber about in spacesuits. Because of the limitations of inexperience, it is difficult for the non-moon walkers to understand when moon walkers discuss it. Those who have first-hand experience of war, such as soldiers, nurses, civilians, and some journalists, may find it impossible to convey their sense of the experience to those who have not been there. This is not because the senders are inarticulate but because the recipients cannot imagine, cannot typically associate the information to something they have experienced. Information in the human model is not sterile and neither is the communication process (Schramm). When Schramm expanded the electronic communication model, adding accumulated human experience and feedback (Severin and Tankard), he was attempting to include aspects of our humanity that have potent effects upon our ability to transmit, receive, and interpret information. He was endeavoring to account for our prior experiences, our roles in social settings, and our identities as aspects of any communication system.

Kenneth Boulding (1956/1973) discusses the relevance of accumulated experience in *The Image*. By locating himself in space and time, reflecting upon who he is, what has made him who he is, and what comprises his identity, he defines his knowledge base or his "image." Boulding contends that the image each of us has, our knowledge base, our identity, is composed of our accumulated experiences, interpretations of those experiences and the effects of the total of our experiences. Essentially, we are the product of our past environment, education, experiences, and we filter all information through these. If you were raised in West Texas, where there are sand dunes, desert scrub brush, and the trees that are rarely taller than the house, you may find it hard to imagine the giant redwoods of northern California or the enormous pines of the northeastern Atlantic seaboard. You might not find it possible to envision twelve-foot high drifts from lake effect snow near Buffalo, New York. The experience of a hurricane would not be yours so long as you remained in West Texas, although you would probably be very familiar with tornadoes and dust storms. Though you may have vicarious information, having seen a film or read a book, the information content, its integration into your being would not be the same as if you had experienced these activities.

In some ways, we all remain naive, limited by the boundaries of our experiences and those who first contributed to our image. We see and perceive the world through what we have already known. What we have not known, or cannot associate to something similar, we may ignore or create an artificial association for, or allow someone else to "give" us an association for it. Our image is composed of the information that has been communicated to us from all the various sources possible and dealt with by us in relation to where this information fits into our image. Some of this image may be the genetic or bio-chemical product of our heritage. Our personal chemistry may impact our infor-mation receptivity, such as when one is depressed or intoxicated. We associate with people who are like us. We do not intentionally spend time with people who hold political views completely opposite of ourselves. We spend time with peo-ple who enjoy the same activities, the same sports, or the same music. We tend not to interact closely with people with whom we have not established some minimal sense of community. "A fundamental principle of human communica-tion is that the exchange of ideas occurs most frequently between individuals who are alike, or homophilous" (Rogers, 1995, p. 286). Our image/identity is our past as well as our present, and it can influence our future. Our image in-cludes the people with whom we associate or identify, our cultural and social identities, and even social customs. This image has a significant effect upon our personal information and communications systems and actions.

An example of the role of social and cultural identity and its capacity to in-fluence our communication and information behavior can be found in diffu-sion research. Everett Rogers' *Diffusion of Innovation* reviewed more than 500 studies about the movement of new ideas, or innovations into general accep-tance with the intent of finding the "common threads running through all the research traditions on the diffusion of innovation" (1995, p. 6). An innovation is information new to a particular setting or individual, regardless of the actual novelty of the information to another individual or in another setting. Diffu-sion of the new information (innovation) is the process or path of communi-cation of the information. The process is influenced by circumstances govern-ing the transmitter, the person initially having the information, the person(s) receiving the information, the recipients and the channels or social/cultural en-vironments surrounding the individuals involved, as well as the content of the information message. Time is also a factor in this process. Individuals may adopt innovations at different rates, often related to their position in the so-cial/cultural environment and other characteristics not yet understood.

Adoption of an innovation is the integration of the information or activity into common use or acceptance. Rogers' (1995) review of works suggested that the social/cultural environment has significant influence upon the adop-tion of innovations. His work also identified categories of adopters based upon their speed of adoption. An aspect of his work that is especially relevant here are cultural norms: common patterns of behavior, conduct, or belief within a social system. These patterns may even be how one cultural group differenti-ates itself from another. At a global level, Christians are those who believe Je-sus Christ is the Supreme Being; at a much more local cultural level, the de-tails of that belief can be substantially different. Consider two Christian groups, the Baptist faith in comparison to the Lutheran faith. In fact, unless you are a student of theology, or have friends in both faiths, you may not have sufficient knowledge about their beliefs to make a comparison. Such is the limitation of social/cultural environments and norms.

In the context of social/cultural norms, these patterns may not only define groups, but may define information acceptability for members of the groups. You are more likely to accept information as valid from someone you know than someone you do not know. You are more likely to listen to the ideas of people you respect or with whom you agree than with the ideas of people whom you do not respect or agree (Haslam, McGarty and Turner, 1996; Rogers, 1995). Think of your political affiliation—do you often find yourself agreeing with the members of other political parties? Do not the relationships you have with people influence how you value or devalue their opinions and ideas? The point being, one's position in a social system and relationship to others does influence what information you accept (Rogers). If you politically identity yourself as a Republican, you are saying you basically believe and subscribe to the political agenda that party espouses. Depending on how closely your personal political views coincide with the party view, how closely your image places you in this system, you may find yourself unable to believe events presented by someone who is not of the Republican party, especially about topics considered to differentiate Republicans from Democrats. Effectively, all political information coming to you is filtered through this image and is affected by your perception of the sender. If the sender is a Republican she or he is likely to affirm what you already believe, or if they challenge it, they will be given the opportunity to communicate. Alternately, if the sender is a Democrat, regardless of what they suggest, you are likely to doubt and/or even disregard the communication. This is not to suggest that there is no reasoning or thinking involved in this, but rather the information from a member of your own group is given more credibility than that of a nonmember. In fact, some studies indicate that even information typically resisted by an individual may be received more openly if presented by someone from their identity group, but there seems to be a conscious evaluation involved regardless of the source (Haslam, McGarty and Turner). Another situation where an outsider's information may be accepted, as suggested by Boulding (1956/1973), would be if somehow the information or communication creates an emotional state, which may make the recipient receptive to information that normally conflicts with their image.

Methods of communication, such as choice of channel, direct or indirect, demonstrative or passive, may also influence whether you accept information. Are you likely to believe someone means you well if they are yelling at you and using abusive language? This is not to imply that we never communicate or accept information from those unlike us. Indeed much the opposite; we do communicate and accept information from people not like us, but our rate of acceptance or our agreement with the information is not the same as when dealing with communicants who are culturally or socially similar. The acceptability of the information, how closely it resembles something we already believe or accept, also contributes.

Boulding (1956/1973) suggests there are three general responses the image may experience in response to information: the image may be unaffected;

the image may change slightly; or the image may undergo a very significant change. One's image may remain unaffected by the morning weather report. One's image may be slightly changed by understanding how to operate a computer software program, but that does not really change how one lives or views the world. Firsthand experience of a war, however, may dramatically influence how you view yourself, your faith, and the world; therefore, your image would be significantly impacted. Taken in the context of Rogers' (1995) work, your image also has a place in a social/cultural environment and your receptivity to new information is partly formed by that environment's affect on your image. Despite the role of the individual, extraneous information communicated via the social/cultural environment will be received consciously or subconsciously. Perceived information that seems irrelevant will be suppressed or dismissed as "noise"; however, it may remain with the recipient subconsciously, until it has a useful application or emerges as part of a social/cultural experience. All of these components contribute to who you are and consequently how willingly you accept information, regardless of the method of communication.

## Communication and Information Transfer

How do the concepts of uncertainty, information, communication, Schramm's model of communication, Boulding's image, Rogers' innovations, and social/cultural environments all tie together? These are all concerns that must be included in any information transfer model; that is, in any communication system. Schramm added accumulated experience and feedback to the model because we interpret whatever is communicated to us through the veil of our past experiences, through our image as Boulding suggests, and because we evaluate and respond more critically to information that seems contrary to our social/cultural environment or social groups belief (Boulding, 1973; Haslam, McGarty and Turner, 1996; Rogers, 1995; Schramm, 1973). The transfer of information then is going to be limited or accentuated by characteristics of the participants, their perceptions of themselves, the presenters, and the information presented. The quality of the information transferred may be modified by these perceptions.

Communication is one of the processes or methods for making information available. Information may reduce uncertainty. But, our image, as explained by Boulding (1956/1973), and our position in a given social or cultural information situation impact what information we will consider accepting into our belief system. The combination of who we believe ourselves to be, who we believe our peers to be, and the degree of our rigidity of belief in certain social and cultural constraints will contribute to our ability to integrate "new" information into our image, and/or belief system. Communication may be significantly impacted by all the resulting "noise." The noise may be composed of the image, stature, or social position of the sender as well as of the recipient. The noise may be an unconscious bias, as in genderism, ageism, sexism, or racism. The noise may be entrenchment, wherein the participants hold their beliefs as inviolate and cannot accept any deviation or suggestion thereof. The noise may be an inability to comprehend the information, due to physical constraints or intellectual limitations. The sender and the receiver may have social, cultural, identity issues, or physical constraints that will influence the quality of the communication act and the success of the information transfer. Just as an electronic communication system may have physically limiting characteristics that contribute to noise, so too can human communications have physical, social, and environmental limitations. When someone speaks, she or he can only determine if the information transfer has been successful if the feedback from the recipient yields some indication of comprehension. However, the original speaker may be misinterpreting the feedback. Information transfer becomes an extremely complex process, dependent upon the participants, the communication methods and protocols, and the total communication environment. Evaluating the entire information and communication environment may assist in improving information transfer. Determining all the aspects of the environment that require detailed study is still underway as we learn more about information and communication systems and behaviors.

## Summary

The human communication and information transfer model is significantly more complex than the essential electronic communications model Shannon proposed. Accepting that individuals have membership in a social/cultural environment, which also places them in a delimited individual image/identity relationship with themselves and others, has important implications in human communication. The basic electronic model does not adequately portray all the characteristics and aspects that may influence human communication. Information possession and transmission involve a variety of processes, environmental factors and systems, which need to be taken into account when evaluating information and communication structures. It is not sufficient to recognize that there is a relationship between information and communication, the relationship must be explored and evaluated.

# References

Bar-Hillel, Y. 1964. Language and Information: Selected Essays on their Theory and Application. Reading, MA: Addison-Wesley.

Boulding, K. 1956/1973. *The Image.* The University of Michigan Press.

Dervin, B. and Nilan, M. 1986. Information Needs and Uses. *Annual Review of Information Science and Technology* 21:3–35.

Haslam, A. S., McGarty, C. and Turner, J. C. 1996. Salient Group Memberships and Persuasion: The Role of Social Identity in the Validation of Beliefs. In J. L. Nye, and A. M. Brower (Eds.). *What's Social About Social Cognition? Research on Socially Shared Cognition in Small Groups* pp. 29–56. Thousand Oaks, CA: Sage.

Ritchie, D. L. 1991. *Communication Concepts 2: Information.* Newbury Park, CA: Sage.

Rogers, E. 1995. *The Diffusion of Innovation* (4th ed.). New York, NY: The Free Press.

Schramm, W. L. 1973. *Men, Messages, and Media: A Look at Human Communication.* New York: Harper & Row.

Severin, W. J. and Tankard, J. W. Jr. 1992. *Communications Theories: Origins, Methods, and Uses in the Mass Media* (3rd ed.). White Plains, NY: Longman.

Shannon, C. and Weaver, W. 1949. *The Mathematical Theory of Communication.* Urbana: University of Illinois Press.

Shera, J. H. 1983. Librarianship and Information Science. In F. Machlup and U. Mansfield, (Eds.). *The Study of Information: Interdisciplinary Messages* pp. 379–388. New York: Wiley & Son.

Tribus, M. 1983. Thirty Years of Information Theory. In F. Machlup & U. Mansfield (Eds.). *The Study of Information: Interdisciplinary Messages* pp. 475–484. New York: Wiley & Son.

Young, P. 1987. *The Nature of Information.* New York, NY: Praeger.

# Chapter 4

# Information Retrieval

## Introduction

Information retrieval refers to the processes and activities involved with making it possible to obtain information from some source. Currently, it is typically associated with computer-based retrieval, but that is not the only form of information retrieval (Goffman, 1968/1970; Salton, 1982). Even with computerized systems, certain aspects of the overall processes involved must be understood. When we ask someone a purposeful question, we are seeking information and engaging in an act of information retrieval. In the human inquiry it is easy to understand that information retrieval involves forms of communication (Schramm, 1973). It may be less obvious with interactions between human and machine, or human and information systems such as libraries, that there are elements of the communications processes involved.

When we consult someone, we are attempting to retrieve information from that person's collected store of information. A component of retrieval is intimately related to the collection of materials, in particular, whether the collection consulted has the information desired and whether it is retrievable. A collection may hold the desired information, but if it cannot be located, it may as well not be present. The ability to locate an item after it has been stored is based upon the organization and subsequent representation employed to describe it for potential retrieval (Lubetzky and Hayes, 1969/1970; Salton, 1982).

How do we locate information? Association seems to play a large role in cognition and has been a powerful influence in the design of classification systems. When information is collected and stored, the issue of locating a specific item of interest at a later time becomes a major concern (Rowley, 1992; Taylor, 1999). How does one go about finding a book in a library or locating a particular subject or author? How can information within documents, video, or other media be handled so an interested party can access it? What enables the retrieval of information from databases or the Web?

Organization and representation are key components of information retrieval. These are critical aspects of the retrieval equation, but they are impacted by human communication considerations as well as by cognitive judgments. This chapter briefly discusses some aspects of organization and classification and the relationship among information, communication, and retrieval.

## Organization as Access

Why are the fruits and vegetables usually located together in a market? Why not have the apples on the shelf next to the applesauce, apple pie filling, and apple juice? Why not have the market arranged by alphabetic order, first aisle could be all the "A" things, the last aisle all the "Z" things? Why not just unload the trucks and put everything in the store in the order it comes off the truck that day? Why are standard phone books arranged by alphabetic order rather than by numeric order? Simply, it makes it easier to find things if they are organized in some manner. Since fruits and vegetables require refrigeration and are valued for their freshness as well as appearance, it seems reasonable to keep them together, usually on countertop displays to maximize the refrigeration and presentation. They are also usually sorted into fruit, with all the apples next to one another, all the pears next to one another, while the vegetables are also grouped together, such as red, yellow, and white onions and different squashes together and so on. This is organization by association. But why not put all the apples with the applesauce and the apple juice? Are the applesauce and the apple juice next to one another on the shelf? Depending on the organization of the market perhaps, but it is just as likely the juices are all together; the fruit sauces are all together. There may be rows of apple juice next to rows of grape juice.

If the store were arranged alphabetically, there would have to be agreement about what each item would be called. It would mean bandages and birdseed would be on the same aisle, as would baloney, bananas, baby powder, and buttons. It could work, except where would facial tissue be put since most people call it by a particular brand name? Should the shelves be arranged alphabetically by the brand name, then the common name? Some brands are regional, some national, some international, and not all stores carry all brands. What about unloading the truck and leaving it in the order of the truck today? What if every truck is not packed in the same order? Every day, things would be in a different order, at least compared to the things unloaded the day before, how would anyone find anything?

There are, of course, phone books arranged by the phone number, it is a reverse phone book for locating who belongs to a number; but the standard phone book works using the alphabet because the user is most likely to know the person's name rather than his or her number. These may seem silly and unimportant, except consider how much time would be wasted in that market where every day there was a different arrangement. How would one look up a phone number if the only information available is the last name? Essentially, without an organizational scheme large collections become inaccessible. The same principles apply to information collections.

Organization, the imposition of some structure, improves one's ability to locate things. In the context of information containers, such as books, newspapers, correspondence, films, videos, computer files, and the many mediums now available, organization is critical to being able to locate information. By imposing a structure, preferably one with clear criteria for inclusion, with rules for placement and association, a blueprint is created that permits the location of items based on the rules that position them in the collection. Additionally, agreed upon rules and criteria for placement make retrieval possible by other than the original organizer (Rowley, 1992). If the organization of a collection of books is agreed to be all paperback books together, alphabetically by author's last name, then we only need to know that the book is available in paper and the author's last name. However, what if the author has a compound last name or no last name? This consideration should be documented and a rule for how to locate that book in the collection should be recorded. What of the hardbound books: should they also be alphabetized by the author's last name? It could work. However, what if you do not know the author's last name? What if you want a book about a particular subject?

A blueprint based on only a few physical characteristics of a book are not sufficient to locate items by subject. In fact, now the problem of location becomes much larger. If there are many books and many subjects, how can the subjects of the book be located without physically examining each book each time there is an interest? One method is to use a surrogate, something that provides information about the book but is not the book, such as a piece of paper, a card, or an entry in a computer file. But then there still needs to be a way to connect the book to the surrogate for the surrogate to refer to the physical book in a specific location (Rowley, 1992). What if the book is about more than one subject? What if it has information that might be useful in a variety of subjects? Using a surrogate system, it is possible to have several cards or such referencing the one book. But how does one determine what the book is about and where it should be positioned in the collection relative to the other members of the collection?

Since Plato, it has been theorized that there is a natural order that should provide a framework for the organization of all knowledge. This framework would provide an arrangement from the general to the specific; that entities would be arranged based upon characteristics similar to each other as well as dissimilarities to other entities, and those characteristics would be essential and unchanging aspects of the entity (Shera, 1965). This hierarchical and relational-based notion of a classification framework continues today, though it is not the only system of organization or classification available.

The impossibility of organizing all knowledge aside, it has been useful to arrange entities by characteristics that define their uniqueness and their similarity in comparison to other entities. For example, vertebrates are creatures with backbones, as opposed to nonvertebrates, which are creatures without backbones. Mammals are warm-blooded vertebrates that give birth to live young to whom they feed milk, as opposed to reptiles, cold-blooded vertebrates that lay eggs and do not feed milk to their offspring. These characteristics or attributes describe the entities in such a way that similarities and differences make it possible to group the entities. The more detailed the characteristics known, the more precisely we can group the entities. Given the information that something is a vertebrate mammal with four legs, (which is really a great deal of information), this indicates the animal has a backbone, has all the characteristics of a mammal, and has four legs. With this information it is clear that the animal is not a human being, nor an amoeba, but it is still not sufficient information to be able to name the animal. Given enough information that it has claws, typically weighs less than twenty pounds, has relatives that are significantly larger, prefers to hunt at night, generally prefers to be solitary, you might be able at some point to guess based upon what you know about animals and their characteristics. There is a scientific classification system that could be employed as well that would describe it: Kingdom: Animalia, Phylum: Chordata, Subphylum: Vertebrata, Class: Mammalia, Order: Carnivora, Family: Felidae, Genus: Felis, Species: Domesticus (Braungart and Buddeke, 1960). Kingdom being the most general of the classifications in this method, and species being the most specific, this is a domestic cat. However, each of the groupings—kingdom, phylum, subphylum, class, order, family, genus, species—indicates certain similarities and differences for the creature to fit into each group level. This means it is possible to locate where an animal belongs in the classification using knowledge of the animal combined with the criteria of each group.

This type of hierarchy has inherited attributes; that is, the characteristics of the higher group appear in the lower level group. All members of the family of Felidae are carnivorous, mammals with backbones. Such a structure also means it is possible to locate related animals at different levels of relationship. For example, there are characteristics that are criteria for belonging to the class mammal and to the order carnivore, only animals with certain specific characteristics will be in the mammal class and carnivore order. However, unless we are familiar with this scientific naming convention, we would not recognize either the hierarchy or the implications of each group level and this classification method might not yield any useful information. This does not change that this classification system does present significant information to those versed with it, and it does provide a way of identifying entities based upon like and unlike attributes. Botany uses the same hierarchical, kingdom-to-species approach to classify plants.

The hierarchical grouping system based on relationships, likeness, and unlikeness has some shortcomings. What characteristics form the basis for the evaluation of the relatedness, likeness, and unlikeness? Should all four-legged creatures be grouped together, or should only warm-blooded, four-legged creatures be grouped together? Should all the aspects of any discipline that has anything to do with information be grouped under information science? Are all blonde-haired children related to each other? Using too few characteristics makes it difficult to usefully arrange items and limits access to the structure by dictating what information the user must have to employ the system. Further, there is an underlying question of the value of relating items on certain characteristics. One would not assume all blonde-haired children are all related. Would there be any value in grouping all blonde children together as a category based upon this criteria? It would depend upon what information was being sought and what other attributes or characteristics were being considered. Other methods of classification might be more meaningful or more flexibly applied.

Criteria for organizing, whether surrogates, physical objects, or ideas, have to be based upon the intended use of the materials and the anticipated users. They have to take into account what descriptive or relationship information is available about the entities and how useful is organizing the material based on those criteria. The organizational structure has to have the capacity to expand, the flexibility to provide multiple access points, and be reflective of the intended users' cognitive levels and interests (Loucopoulos, 1992; Mylopoulos, 1992; Rolland and Cauvet, 1992; Rowley, 1992).

The application of organizational criteria is part of providing access, that is, creating a method for pulling information out of a collection. If all books bound in blue were about law enforcement, then putting all the blue books together would place all the law enforcement volumes in one place. If you knew all the blue books were about this one subject and you needed information about that subject you would only examine the blue books, not the red, not the black, nor the green. If the blue books were also arranged alphabetically by the last name of the author, then it might not be necessary to examine all the blue books if you knew the author's last name. However, if you only knew the title, you would still have to look at each book, unless the books were arranged by title instead of author.

Since an item can only be in one place and the arrangement of the books is not likely to change based on what we do or do not know, the use of the surrogate becomes more powerful. In theory, many surrogates can be created to refer to the one item based upon the method of description. The method of description, the classification, has to be agreed upon. That is, each surrogate for each item in the collection will have sufficient information to distinguish one item from another. It would also be very helpful if each surrogate used an agreed-upon reference for locating the item in space. For example, before electronic databases, the access points to a library collection were defined by the catalog card system, a card being a record and a document surrogate. Each card had a referent number, or call number, which was a method for locating the item on the shelf. Each document had as many card records as the system determined appropriate. Typically a title card, author card, and some subject cards. Each of these cards would be an access point; if one knew the title or the author, or had an idea of the subject, it was possible to locate the document. The cards basically became a database of entries descriptive of the contents of the collection. Each surrogate card was a record referring to an item in the collection.

In electronic database construction, the records are composed of fields or categorized characteristics, which describe the physical entity, or subject entity, to which the record refers. For example, documentary materials are classified using characteristics such as title words, citations and references, subject keywords, and author. These are characteristics or attributes that describe the document. In a database, the record for such an entity might be retrievable by any of the fields, or attributes, depending upon the design of the retrieval system and the database. The record would refer back to the actual document, as in how to locate it via a document number, a journal citation, or call number. Other types of collections are characterized by attributes that describe the basic collection entities, or subjects of the database, such as customer databases. The customer is the entity or subject, and attributes are the aspects that describe the customer, such as address, purchasing history, income, gender, age, and so on. How well the attributes describe, or represent, the entity and the relationship of that representation to the user's knowledge base will significantly impact the user's ability to retrieve the appropriate record using the attributes as access points. If we are seeking information about cats, and the attributes for animals are all in Latin, if we do not know Latin, then the records cannot be located.

## Organization, Details, and Retrieval

To implement an organization and classification system requires agreement about the criteria and their application: the definition of the vocabulary to be employed, the methods for selecting the content of an item, and the format of presentation for the records. Details as to how to determine the subjects, attributes, or descriptors of items have to be established. What will be the primary entities, the most useful descriptors, what depth of detail should be employed? In a documentary system, will subjects be determined by frequency of meaningful words and/or phrases or derived from titles and abstracts? In a customer database, will the primary entry be the customer, the item purchased, the account number, the sales contact, or a combination of these? Should the record be kept in a numerically coded format or natural language or a combination of both? All of these questions need answers.

The details required to make organization and classification schemes useful are numerous and usually create a complex artificial structure. These schemes are then applied to a collection that produces an imposed structural organization that should allow for information to be retrieved by applying an understanding of the structure via an inquiry system. In a library catalog card system, the user searches by looking in the card file via the access points, the author, title, or subject file, depending upon what information the user has available. The user seeking information is actively undertaking an inquiry. This user may be seeking a specific book or additional information about a specific subject. In another environment the user might be trying to trace a purchase order or a customer billing address. The searcher's ability to manipulate the system will be dependent upon how well the information entered into the system complies with the structure and how well the user understands the structure and the scheme. The ability to retrieve information from the collection will be dependent on how well the organizational structure is understood and how the subject of interest is represented in that structure. Historically, the use of classification structures has resulted in using intermediaries especially trained with the systems imposed, or training users in how to use specific systems successfully. The lack of generality in systems has sometimes required significant investment in training with every advance in technology.

Classification and organization schemes may limit access points trying to uniformly implement the scheme. The access points may have been identified by people who are not experts in the given discipline. When determining a subject for a document, experts in the field may have a different orientation than novices or librarians, and this can cause difficulties. For example, when a user is subject searching a library catalog, the subject identification is limited to what is selected by the cataloging department. This sometimes means the user has to outguess the catalogers to locate an item, or rely upon the catalogers' interpretation of a subject area. The use of thesauri, indexes, and "see also" help with this problem but do not ameliorate it. Recent research, however, suggests subject experts do not achieve significantly improved retrieval over nonexperts (Wilbur, 1998), which would lead to the conclusion that the need for catalogers to have extensive subject knowledge may have been an erroneous assumption. It does not negate the need to train users in specific database retrieval systems or interfaces to achieve results. While library organizational schemes have a history and a certain amount of uniformity to the application of classification and description, no such constraints direct other types of databases.

In early electronic databases, space and memory limited the number of access points, thereby leaving the user still highly dependent upon the skills of the database designers and programmers. The controlled structure of a classification scheme, or controlled vocabulary, encouraged the application of information technology. Machines can manipulate controlled vocabulary and follow rules with less effort than is required to handle natural language. Machine limitations and the advantages of classification schemes affected early database design from both input and retrieval perspectives. Space and memory limitations restricted the quantity and method in which information could be stored. Information was abbreviated and arranged to maximize space savings; coupled with the characteristics of the schema used, the need for intermediaries was perpetuated. In library settings, the most visible databases were the Online Public Access Catalogs (OPAC) and the vendored databases rendered via DIALOG- or LEXIS-NEXIS-like corporations. The vendored database access offered by the library translated into library staff accepting information inquiries from patrons, inventing strategies to query the databases, and offering the result to the patron who would determine relevance. Behind the scenes, databases supported the acquisitions, circulation, and administration requirements of the facility. These were also limited by structures imposed at the database design stage, which ideally should have incorporated an organization and descriptive system appropriate to the specific intended uses. In nonlibrary organizations, the intermediaries would be data processing personnel, programmers, and analysts, who would implement information requests via programming, or searchers trained to use the databases. The retrieval of personnel, customer, payment, circulation, vendor, and acquisition records is as dependent upon the adequacy of the organization and representation as documentary records and in some cases perhaps more significantly. A document record that misdirects the user is hardly as important as a personnel record that misdirects a check, social security, or tax payment information.

## Designing for Retrieval

There are several factors involved in the design of any information retrieval system. The intent or purpose of the collection for how the information will be used will affect the structure of the database, the formats for storage, input and output, the design of the user interface (the computer screens, card catalogs, or whatever method the user interacts with the system), and other issues such as security and currency. What characteristics of the information will be most useful to satisfy the intention will contribute to the structure of the database, as well as influence formats and input and output. Who will be the users, and what characteristics about them may have an influence on the system? This question seeks information specific to the application and its relationship to the users, and the users to the application, all of which may require attention in the design of the system at all levels.

The use of the collection is important in the design because it will indicate what information and what formats of information are needed to build the collection. In the context of a database, what information is to be stored in records and what attributes will be employed to best describe the primary entity the record is intended to reflect? The planned application of the database should influence these decisions. Will natural language or controlled vocabulary be used to place information into the system? Natural language, or language the way humans normally speak or write, has nuances and meanings that are affected by context and a degree of currency, which makes it more difficult for computers to use and may require more manipulation or programming at the interface and storage level to make it work transparently for the user. Where is the information coming from? Will it be downloaded from another source, or will it be collected over time and input as it arrives? This influences the format for input and any interface display consideration. Who collects the information, verifies it if necessary, and evaluates the integrity of the input could also impact the format of the record as well as the interface.

Another important question is what characteristics of the information will be most useful to satisfy the purpose of the collection? These characteristics establish the parameters for the information set to be collected and may also define the structure to be employed. Concerns, such as any space limitations, may contribute to selecting the most useful characteristics and omitting others judged as less critical. The potential for overlooking an essential piece of information is much higher when there are constraints such as space, language, or input features. Within the limitations of the technology, as much flexibility as possible should be built into the structure, and decisions about potentially useful information have to be made. As technology has improved there has been a movement toward data warehousing, storing information collected in the normal process of business or operations. These collections may be enormous. In these cases it is difficult to anticipate what information may be extracted from the warehouse in the future, but it further underlines the importance of planning for flexibility.

Who will the users be: technicians, students, minimum wage transient employees, programmers, designers, salesclerks? Just as communication may be impacted by the "image" and social/cultural environment of the sender and receiver, so too will information retrieval. The reasons users are attempting to retrieve information, their motivation, their concept of how to use the system and their measure of what they are seeking are all critical to the retrieval process. In fact, it will be the users who ultimately determine whether the retrieval activity, regardless of its intention, is successful; does it resolve or address the information request they posed? The structures created to organize information to make it accessible may also contribute to the complex problem of locating information. The ease of use will impact whether the user views the retrieval activity as successful. The user's competence with the system may impact the sense of success, as does the determination of whether the retrieval addresses the request. If the user is not competent with a system, they may have difficulty obtaining results, even though the desired information may actually be within the system. Another issue will be relevance, or the "aboutness" of the item retrieved. Is it related, connected, relevant to the information inquiry? The user's competence in the area of the information request will impact whether the user perceives the retrieved results as being related to the inquiry (Gluck, 1995). The individual's skills, image, social/cultural interpretation of the transaction will affect the retrieval of desired information and the ability of the individual to recognize the information as relevant.

## Concepts of Relevance

An aspect of information retrieval under extensive study involves the notions of relevance, how individuals determine whether an information item is pertinent, useful, or about the information need they are seeking to re-solve. Research into what components of an information unit trigger a per-ception of relevance indicates a wide variety of factors at play. The infor-mation need is situationally and contextually dependent. The importance of the desired information influences the sources consulted. Basic criteria, such as currency, language, even authorship, may be a factor in detecting poten-tial relevance (Barry, 1998). The initial information state of the seeker will affect the determination of relevance by providing initial gross criteria, such as currency and language. Secondary markers for relevance are more vari-able. Barry details twenty categories of potential relevance criteria in docu-ment selection. Like much of the research in relevance, however, the find-ings are not entirely conclusive. The various components of documents that may convey relevance information, ranging from titles and abstracts to final paragraphs, all elicit differing degrees of usefulness in the evaluation of rel-evance. Barry points out that the context of the search, as well as the user's previous knowledge of both the topic and the sources, may influence the ef-fective detection of relevant items. It would appear that the complexity of the information need, the environment, user, and information item may make it impossible to create a definitive key field for relevance evaluation. Regard-less of that possibility, identifying relevance markers may contribute to en-hanced retrieval systems.

## Summary

The retrieval of information is dependent upon organization or classifi-cation systems. The degree of success to be obtained from these systems will be based upon their relevance to the users and the representativeness imbedded in the scheme used for the subject area. These systems have to be bound to the knowledge environments, which the information seekers in the subject domain can implement to recall materials relevant to their inquiries. The activities of pulling useful information out of a collection are con-nected to the organizational scheme and to relationships invoked via the in-quiry. Whether technologically based or not, the construction and applica-tion of a classification system must take into account the users. The parameters of the users' abilities, the relationships employed to construct the classification, and the representativeness of the descriptions all impact how well a retrieval system can satisfy the users' needs. Organization of materials should be viewed as a method of access. Coupled with criteria to establish relevance, or aboutness, for the user in conjunction with the col-lection structures resulting from classification, it should be possible to pro-vide a working retrieval system.

In the electronic environment, selection becomes a more individualized task. If more criteria for selection are to be applied, more ways to examine, evaluate, classify, organize and represent materials must be developed. With more sophisticated searching tools, at least in theory, users could better frame their inquires and obtain better results with less attention from intermediaries. Since information retrieval relevance is a user-dependent activity, it seems logical to increase the users' ability to apply a system directly.

# References

Barry, C. 1998. Document Representations and Clues to Document Relevance. *Journal of the American Society for Information Science.* 49(14):1293–1303.

Braungart, D. C. and Buddeke, R. 1960. *An Introduction to Animal Biology* (5th ed.). St. Louis, MO: C. V. Mosby.

Fayyad, U. 1996. Data Mining and Knowledge Discovery: Making Sense Out of Data. *IEEE Expert* 11(5):220–225.

Fayyad, U., Piatetsky-Shapiro, G. and Smyth, P. 1996. From Data Mining to Knowledge Discovery in Databases. *Ai Magazine* 17(3):3754.

Foskett, A. C. 1977. *The Subject Approach to Information* (3rd ed.). Hamden, CT: Linnet Books, The Shoe String Press.

Gluck, M. 1995. Understanding Performance in Information Systems: Blending Relevance and Competence. *Journal of the American Society for Information Science* 46(6):446–460.

Goffman, W. 1968/1970. An Indirect Method of Information Retrieval. In T. Saracevic, (Ed.). *Introduction to Information Science* pp. 485–492. New York, NY: R. R. Bowker.

Loucopoulos, P. 1992. Conceptual Modeling. In P. Loucopoulos and R. Zicari, (Eds.) *Conceptual Modeling, Databases and CASE: An Integrated View of Information Systems Development* pp. 1–26. New York, NY: John Wiley & Sons.

Lubetzky, S. and Hayes, R. M. 1969/1970. Bibliographic Dimensions in Information Control. In T. Saracevic, (Ed.). *Introduction to Information Science* pp. 434–444. New York, NY: R. R. Bowker.

Mylopoulos, J. 1992. Conceptual Modeling and Telos. In P. Loucopoulos and R. Zicari, (Eds.). *Conceptual Modeling, Databases and CASE: An Integrated View of Information Systems Development* pp. 49–68. New York, NY: John Wiley & Sons.

Rolland, C. and Cauvet, C. 1992. Trends and Perspectives in Conceptual Modeling. In P. Loucopoulos and R. Zicari, (Eds.) *Conceptual Modeling, Databases and CASE: An Integrated View of Information Systems Development* pp. 27–48. New York, NY: John Wiley & Sons.

Rowley, J. 1992. *Organizing Knowledge: An Introduction to Information Retrieval* (2nd ed.). Brookfield, VT: Ashgate.

Salton, G. 1982. Information Retrieval: An Introduction. In *Introduction to Modern Information Retrieval* pp. 1–23. New York, NY: McGraw-Hill.

Shera, J. H. 1965. *Libraries and the Organization of Knowledge.* Foskett, D. J., (Ed.). Hamden, CT: Archon Books.

Shera, J. H. 1966. *Documentation and the Organization of Knowledge.* Foskett, D. J., (Ed.). Hamden, CT: Archon Books.

Taylor, A. G. 1999. *The Organization of Information.* Englewood, CO.: Libraries Unlimited.

Wilbur, W. J. 1998. A Comparison of Group and Individual Performance among Subject Experts and Untrained Workers at the Document Retrieval Task. *Journal of the American Society for Information Science* 49(6):517–529.

# Chapter 5

# Bibliometrics

## Introduction

Bibliometrics uses quantitative and qualitatively descriptive methods, such as statistics and mathematical analysis, to examine documents. However, the study of bibliometrics is also concerned with document surrogates, the relations that might be derived or inferred related to the production, manipulation or redistribution of information (Buckland, 1991; Pao, 1989; White and McCain, 1989). The word bibliometrics can be divided into "biblio," which refers to books or bibliographies, and "metrics," which refers to measurement. Bibliometrics references the various methodologies of measurement applied to the artifacts of human communication forms, previously thought of primarily as books, or other textual representatives. This very broad definition is intended to include new information and communication forms such as databases and other methods of recording information as well as not limit the notion of bibliometrics to bibliographies, or only physical print materials.

Human information is stored in a variety of media amenable to measurement, including text, film, electronic, aural recordings, art, and other recordable or translatable formats. Some researchers separate the study of information and communication forms into separate groups such as data, information, knowledge, and documents or text (Lewis and Jones, 1996). But the application of bibliometric techniques has implications for all of these states. Using basic quantification methods may identify patterns of word use, vocabulary, or syntactic structures. Locating high or low frequency occurrences of specific phrases, words, or structures may indicate an area worthy of further exploration. Recurring patterns in data, subject, queries, citations, authorship, publication data, themes, characters, etc., may suggest researchable issues or relationships.

Concepts and methodologies from bibliometrics are now found in applications of data mining as a component of knowledge discovery in databases (KDD). Retrospective examination of database collections to identify any potential patterns or statistically significant variations may yield new insight into the objects of the database or yield construction and relationships within the database and possibly the entities the database represents (Fayyad, Piatetsky-Shapiro and Smyth, 1996). Bibliometrics investigates information and communication via a variety of quantifications, such as frequency of occurrence of specific words, phrases, citations, co-citation, publications, authorship and related characteristics as potential aspects of content analysis or evaluation. It may be applied to detect patterns such as authorship in a field, in citations, in phrase usage, or publications. Bibliometrics may be used to identify title clusters, journal clusters, discipline, and diffusion networks. The practical uses of bibliometrics include contributing information for decision making regarding collection development, weeding, cataloging and classification, circulation patterns, and much more. Bibliometrics is both a research and practical tool. This chapter will overview some of the key notions of bibliometrics and its applications in various roles.

## Measurement, Description, and Information

Measurement provides a method for describing an entity. How tall a tree is, how many rings in the trunk, the depth of its bark, or the number of leaves on a stem, all contribute to describing the tree and may also allow for inferences about its age or its relationship to other plants. How many books in a library collection relate a description of size. A count of how many books in a specific subject area and published in a given time period provides more descriptive information, which could permit inferences to be made about the library's use, patrons or collection development policies. The basis of all science and research comes from observation, one intent of observation is description, which may include measurement as a method.

Sometimes it is difficult to ascertain the appropriate method of measurement. For example, there is much debate about a proper method to measure student achievement or teaching success. If grades measure student achievement, should grades given by teachers be considered the measure of the success of their teaching? The question becomes what do grades measure, and what do those measurements mean? If all of a teacher's students are given "A," does that mean the teacher is successful? Since the teacher awards the grades there may be a conflict in looking at success from this view (not to suggest teachers give grades for any reason other than correct completion of syllabus requirements). Just because there are measurements, does not mean they are appropriate or informative; the context and criteria must be clear and fit what is being examined.

Observation and description are research processes, not just measurement activities, and measurement is not sufficient to assure comprehension of an occurrence. Amount does not correlate to quality, and it is not acceptable to make inferences about quality based entirely on quantity. How many articles an author has published yields no information about the quality of those articles. How frequently an author is cited does not necessarily translate into a statement of quality, or even expertise. An author may be cited frequently for a number of reasons, including that many other authors disagree with his or her writings. How frequently an author publishes does provide information about his or her productivity but not about the quality of the product. How frequently an author is cited does suggest how widely read the author may be, regardless of the quality of the writing.

Measurement supplies descriptive information, such as how frequently a word is used or how frequently an author publishes. Measurement permits comparisons based on quantity, frequency, length, and even characteristics of quality. Bibliometrics provides measurements and descriptions from the study of our information, communication records, and literature. Pao suggests that bibliometric studies deal with three components, "1) the physical object . . . 2) its creation and subject content; and 3) its use" (1989, p.14). The physical object currently would include electronic communications and media, such as radio, television, film, e-mail, e-journals, e-publications, tape, CD, and the like, which are "captured" or recorded in some manner that permits retrospective examination and evaluation. Creation and content evaluations would examine the productivity of authors, currency of content, content coverage, and spread of content. Studying uses and users is possibly the most complex of bibliometric concerns, as there are compound factors involved that seem to defy quantification, such as human information seeking behavior. These three broad classifications of study for bibliometrics actually represent a multitude of smaller investigative areas and applications. These studies have the potential to reveal maps of literature or communication: who cites whom, who co-cites suggest discipline foci and interest groups, paths of information exchange or communication networks. Article titles in journals may indicate subfields, or areas of interest for the journal or the journal sponsors. Bibliometric studies may suggest trends in authorship, publication, subject coverage, growth in a discipline, or ideas. Using techniques such as Bradford's core and scatter, bibliometrics may identify the journal's key to providing the most comprehensive cover of a topic using the least number of journals. Computer algorithms can be applied to create indexes based on word frequency and scaled rankings. The application of bibliometric techniques can be used in document-retrieval systems, acquisition programs, circulation statistics, and even user preferences. Various database records reviewed retrospectively may reveal purchasing patterns among clients, banking practice habits in regions, health and disease patterns among the clientele of an insurance agent or large employee system, or no patterns at all. Bibliometrics encompasses a wide variety of methods of analysis based upon the record of information and communication.

## Measurement: Objects and Representatives of Information

One area of bibliometrics examines aspects of the objects or representatives of information exchange. One method evaluates the history of the objects, that is, how many of these objects are produced now versus previously? More precisely, how many of $x$ objects in $y$ context are produced now versus previously? For example, how many electronic articles are published in juried electronic journals in the field of library and information science in 2000, how many in 1995? As in any attempt at description and measurement criteria, parameters need to be clearly indicated to ensure only those items that are intended to be counted or measured are included and everything else excluded. Clearly there are requirements involved in the previous inquiry; electronic articles are a relatively new publication form. Juried electronic journals are not only a specific journal format but also have a very selective inclusion policy. Limiting the discipline to library and information science further restricts the items eligible to be included in the count and also creates the parameters that will allow us to have meaningful discussion of the results, as does the inclusion of time periods. Only electronically published articles in juried electronic journals from the field of library and information science would be counted. They would be counted by year, from 1995 through 2000. If there was a statistically significant change in the number of electronic articles published in juried e-journals of library and information science, it might be useful to seek adjunct information that might have influenced the change. Regardless of what numeric results were obtained by pursuing this query, it would be essential to note factors surrounding the time period involved, the prevalence in general of juried electronic journals in 1995 versus 2000, the tenure criteria acceptable in 1995 regarding electronic publication versus print publication compared to 2000, and so on.

The numeric results of the analysis form only a partial basis for exploration but also contribute to laying a foundation and may suggest other territories requiring exploration. A practical application of information such as this would be to review the journal collection policy for this field of study to determine whether the increase in juried e-journals has impacted the print journals. Further study would be necessary to determine whether topics covered in the e-journals are the same as those covered in print journals. Has there been any change in the number, quality, or coverage of the print journals; are the e-journals just another format or are they replacing the print journals? These are critical questions from a collection development and budget point of view, which may make use of bibliometric study results.

Another example of measuring objects or representatives would be researching the number of journals published in medicine between 1899 and 1999—how many were published each year, were there changes in the number of journals published, were there changes in the number of journals in a specific language, were there any changes in the number or identity of publishers of these journals, and so on. This type of study provides information about the growth of records in a field and might suggest transformations in the field itself. Further, it provides estimates of the continuing growth patterns and the implications of such upon the collecting libraries, including predicting future shelf space and storage problems. Changes in publication patterns can be indicative of larger economic changes, shifts in formats, interests, and business strength. If the primary language of publication changes, could that suggest a change in a discipline's core group? Sometimes measuring and observing create more questions to consider rather than resolving any.

A method thought to be practical for evaluating the usefulness of specific journals examines citation half-life and use half-life. Citations are references to another document (using the widest possible definition of document). These references to another document indicate a relationship and suggest that the citing author has consulted the cited document, thereby being a possible measure of use. A suggestion that one author has consulted another's writings may be a means for mapping idea transmission, or interests groups, or nothing at all. Half-life studies attempt to evaluate the length of time in which a journal is used, either as a resource as indicated by citation, or physical use as indicated by circulation (Pao, 1989). Tsay (1998) examines journal "life" based on uses as demonstrated by circulation and citation. The premise of half-life in bibliometrics is to determine when half of all the active literature of a field has been published, or the time period that includes half or more of the references made. Short half-life, whether citation based or use based, which means more than 50 percent of the use or citations occurred in a short period of time, implies "new volumes of a title are generally used more often than older volumes" (Tsay, p. 1285). Half-life studies may suggest which journals are most used, but may also exaggerate use in that there are more publications now than previously. There have been suggestions that half-life studies could identify which journals are least used, resulting in a list of items to consider for discontinuation. Caution should be taken in applying such a plan; the mission of the institution, the orientation and behavior of the users, and any possible other contributors to low use, such as inaccessibility, should be considered.

Citation analysis may be used to identify the most discussed issues in a field and topic area. It may also be a way to establish what the focus of interests, or new topics, in a discipline were at a given time or the influences affecting the field. Dumas (1993) used a combination of citation analysis and subject classification to examine and characterize the British and United States social work literature published between 1984 and 1991. He was seeking to identify the core themes of that literature and any changes or trends that might be evident though an evaluation of the citations. Such information may be valuable when attempting to ensure inclusiveness of a collection. The study was also significant for applying bibliometric techniques to social work literature.

## Measurements: Creation and Content

Another measure using citations involves counting the number of times a specific article or author is cited. This may indicate that it has some authority on a subject, that the item is central to a discipline area, or even that it is a topic of a significant debate. The number of times an author is cited may indicate he or she is an authority in an area, is a prolific author, is controversial, or a primary source for some topic. Occasionally, the number of times an author is cited has been looked upon as an estimate of his or her stature or scholarly importance in a field. This is not an appropriate measure of scholarly success, as even a fool may be cited frequently in order to refute his writing.

Author productivity may be measured by how frequently he or she publishes. A simple count of publications, as mentioned before, does not indicate quality, only quantity. However, it is possible to compare frequency of publications among authors within a field. This measurement evaluates the distribution of authorship in a field. Lokta examined *Chemical Abstracts* to determine the number of individual authors and their papers compared to the total number of papers in the period 1907 to 1916. The outcome of this study showed more than 63 percent of the authors in that sample had only one publication, 15 percent had two publications, 7 percent had three publications, 4 percent had four publications, 2 percent had five publications. Authors of six to forty-four publications each represented the balance, that is 9 percent of the authors produced six to forty-four publications each. Later studies of authorship performed on samples from a major university catalog, and another using a sample of Library of Congress MARC records suggest that the number of authors producing one work was between 50 and 75 percent (Vickery and Vickery, 1987). Newer studies might show this productivity relationship has changed. One could theorize a shift in author productivity in recent time with new stress on publications as part of university tenure and funding, but much more sophisticated measures would have to be undertaken to investigate whether a change in the production relationship has occurred. On the other hand, if in reality only a few authors are responsible for the majority of publications, there may be implications for collection development. Vickery suggests it would first mean that having all the authors, including specifically all the single item authors, represented in a collection would be "very arduous" (p. 234). Alternatively, it might be interpreted to mean that collecting only the prolific authors would provide satisfactory coverage of a topic. Again that is not necessarily a good assumption because it negates possibly critical contributions from the single item authors. Quantity is not an indication of quality whether the amount is large or small.

Quantity can convey some information about items that can aid in identifying content. How many times would we have to see the word "cat" in a document to think the document might have something to do with cats? Not that the document is about cats, but just there is some concept or relationship inherent in the document that requires the word "cat" or "cats" more frequently than other words. If you remove all the noncontent bearing words (such as "a," "an," "the," "and," "which," "that," "what," etc.), arrange all the content bearing words with similar meanings together and then by how frequently they occur, it may be possible to ascertain something about the document content. The following list represents such an extraction from a section of a previous chapter. The numeral preceding any word indicates the word appeared in that specific form that many times. The words with associated meaning are grouped together; the semicolons separate the associated groups:

> Two classification systems, 2 classification, 2 organization, descriptions, organizational, scheme, collection structures, criteria, scheme; 2 relationships, 2 relevance, relevant, aboutness; user, 2 users, users' needs, users' abilities, information seekers; recall, 2 retrieval system, retrieval of information; subject area, subject domain; 2 representativeness; 2 systems; inquiries, inquiry; information; knowledge environments; parameters; technologically based.

Note that the most common words have to do with classification, organization, scheme, and structure; the next most common words have to do with relevance, aboutness; the third most common have to do with users; and the fourth most common have to do with retrieval. Based on this list of words could we determine which chapter section the list comes from and what the section was about, or at least guess something about the content? It is not a completely reliable method because language is very complex with several patterns intrinsic to a specific language. People utilize language very differently, but the method has some applications, with constraints.

What is the value of such an activity? Evaluating word and phrase frequencies may provide some insight into the "aboutness" or the subject matter. Phrase frequencies may be specific to disciplines, or word choices may indicate a subdiscipline or sublanguage (Losee and Haas, 1995). Identifying content words can be important in the appropriate classification of an item, in the development of sufficient indexing or cross references, and hence also critical in the retrieval of the item. One of the ways to determine whether a document has any value in resolving a question is by trying to place the content, the aboutness, of the item in relation to the question. If the interest is cats, the summary of phrases indicates the item represented by the phrases above is not likely to be about cats, but rather about classification and organization and possibly retrieval. Hence that item would not be considered as likely to have information about or related to cats.

Citation analysis has also been used to evaluate documents for subject content. The assumption is that having a sufficient number of citations in common, or from a particular topical area, implies the current document must have content relationships with the cited material. If the majority of the citations in a paper are to other documents that are concerned with bibliometrics, then perhaps the paper being evaluated is also concerned with bibliometrics. This is not an adequate determinate of subject content by itself as it does not provide any depth of content description. A paper with many citations related to bibliometrics has something to do with bibliometrics, but what specifically? Is it an overview, a critique, a bibliometric study, or what? Subject analysis is more than a surface estimation of content and requires significantly more investment than mere citation matching.

Tools to assist in locating information, without having to examine an entire document include document surrogates such as catalog records, citations, abstracts, summaries, indexes, database search systems, Web search engines, and more. The implementation of these surrogates in a retrieval attempt is complex and dependent upon both the ability to synthesize the actual document into a representative surrogate and to relate that to retrieval inquiries. For example, the creation of indexes for information retrieval is two pronged; first an item has to be analyzed for subject content, and second, indexing terms reflective of the content of the item have to be selected. Determining the subject content of an item theoretically may be accomplished by examining and distilling the content of a document into representative characteristics. However, when individuals have unique interpretations of the meaning of a document, of what is representative, or of most critical importance in conveying the subject content, it is difficult to be assured even two readers would select the same descriptive terms. Further, there is the issue of whether the terms selected correspond to an investigator's interpretation of a question.

The problems inherent in subject/content analysis have yielded an assortment of schemes to address them, including controlled vocabularies, thesauri, classification systems, bibliometric techniques, and machine indexing using the actual document text (Taylor, 1999). Experiments have been performed using the overlap and transition range of high frequency and low frequency words as indexing terms. A related approach counts word frequencies for each unique word and compares the normalized percentage values to a standard of relative frequency in the language. If the value is higher than the standard, the word may be used for indexing. Another method uses only the top five percent of content bearing words appearing in a ranked frequency list generated from a document to create index terms. It is possible to have computers count words and apply statistical and mathematical schemes to perform automatic indexing. Document relatedness may be evaluated by comparing high frequency words and matching documents with significant similarity in words and occurrence (Pao, 1989). Interest in automatic indexing is now linked to the emergence of the World Wide Web, which is a virtually infinite information space with relatively limited retrieval mechanisms. Methods to identify documents, sites, homepages, or links responsive to a search request are critical to further development of the Web's potential (Chen, Chung, Ramsey and Yang, 1998).

A traditional approach to analyzing documents for content involves examining the components: title and subtitle, table of contents, introduction, any provided index terms, phrases, or figurative content. Characterizing the subject content of the item with terms or phrases from the document that will be representative of the content to a prospective user is critical to future retrieval. Whether placed into a catalog card system or an electronic database, content description of the document must reflect the document. A searcher would rely on the analysis and representativeness of these aspects to locate a document useful to address an information need.

A correspondent system for the Web involves examining the HTML header areas, sometimes searching the entire document by performing a keyword count based on the search keywords input by the user. The application of this type of search and match has encouraged the discussion of metadata fields (data about the data) that could be used to organize the Web. Problems and concerns about the implementation of another artificial structure over the current icon of free flowing information keep the notion of metadata a hot topic. Some proponents suggest authoring software be employed, which allows the creators of Web pages to enter the keywords, descriptors, or whatever metadata they feel relevant at the top of the HTML page. This system has potential and a number of groups are working on it or related ideas (Chowdhury, 1999). Other approaches include intelligent agents that extend the basic counting concepts of bibliometrics by automatically indexing the content of a page and comparing it by using a number of statistical programs to determine the closeness or relatedness of one page to another. Some systems collect URLs (uniform resource locators or Web addresses) of pages that have high keyword counts matching the search inquiry. Then they solicit user evaluation of the retrieved pages to construct a tighter search plan by using the identified pages as models for further matching. The potential for exploring the Web using bibliometric techniques and sophisticated new computing tools is exciting and challenging.

## Bradford's Law

An early bibliometric measure devised by Samuel Bradford has yielded interesting results when it is applied in different venues than he had originally intended. Bradford identified a pattern, in some ways similar to Lokta's discovery about author concentration. A small number of journals in a specific field will contain the highest concentration of articles, while a larger number of journals will have a lower concentration. This "core and scatter" translates into a pattern wherein a small core of journals contain the majority of articles on a given topic. For instance, if one journal contained fifteen articles about information retrieval on the Web, that might be a core journal for that area. If another journal only had ten articles and another had five then it would take those two journals to provide the same number of articles as the core journal. This pattern extends outward, requiring more and more journals to supply fifteen more articles; these are scattered in different zones depending on how many journals in the zone are necessary to obtain fifteen more articles. Bradford theorized that a core of journals and the zones of scatter for a subject could be determined. This permits one to select the fewest journals that would provide the best coverage of a topic. With limited budgets, it would be most economical to purchase the journals with the most concentrated coverage first. Core and scatter type behavior has been noted in journals, in author productivity, and citation frequency as well as other areas. Bradford's law has been applied to a variety of subject areas with similar though not identical results. Research continues to investigate whether there is an underlying rationale for this pattern of dispersion (Pao, 1989).

Core and scatter zones have been the basis for collection development tools used in small or special libraries. For example, using a core and scatter zone list of medical journals, it is possible to identify which journals would be necessary to provide coverage of a specific portion of the field. If the intention is to provide access to two-thirds of the resources of the field, then the journals should be selected from the core and scatter zones that will produce that proportion. Naturally, there are flaws in this approach to collection development; critical research may appear in journals in the outer scatter zones, where it may take fifty journals to yield fifteen articles on the topic. Important ideas are not always readily accepted and may not surface in the core journals until the idea is accepted. Meanwhile, important time has been lost. Companario (1996) found that some articles, which were found to be very highly cited and therefore considered of value to the field, had difficulty being published. The structures in place to maintain the quality of journals may contribute to delaying publication of new or controversial ideas as these may be difficult to verify, posing the potential of ridicule for the publishing body. A journal, having available a large number of articles about a topic by established researchers, may not be interested in publishing the works of lesser known authors, or those with less established reputations, especially if the ideas are controversial. Relying entirely on the core and scatter law may not be desirable, as there are more factors involved in journal publication than Bradford's law necessarily reflects. Core and scatter has important implications, but should be tempered, as should most bibliometric methods, with additional information, more than one measurement system, and common sense based upon the underlying requirements of the collection, facility, or research.

Citation analysis, mentioned briefly earlier, may be used as a method to trace the flow or dissemination of information. Citations reflect connectedness of some form from document to document. When two items are cited together in another item, the first two are considered to be co-cited. Co-citation may represent a link from earlier work to later work, it may suggest common interests among the two cited authors, or it may be a map to joining journal content, dependent upon the frequency of the occurrence of co-citation. Even single citation can be traced document to document, journal to journal, to create a topography of the movement of an article's concepts through a document system or even a field. Following citations over time and across documents may yield information about transfers from theoretical to applied work (van der Wurff, online, March 7, 1997). Tracing citations may indicate the growth of an idea as it matures by use. Co-citations may indicate connections among ideas or interests that might provide different approaches to topics. Using citation analysis can assist in establishing subject interest cohorts and research fronts, as well as identifying potential high yield journals or authors. It has been a topic of debate in the construction of tools to evaluate the usefulness of serials holdings and to validate selection and retention of journals (Calhoun, 1995).

## Measurements: Users and Uses

Research about users and uses of information may be the most complex area of interest to the librarian and information scientist. The level of complexity should be evident by the terminology and its lack of clarity. What is meant by "users" and "uses" of information? It could be demonstrated that everyone "uses" information and therefore is a "user" of information. In attempting to study uses and users, it became apparent that definition would be difficult (Pao, 1989).

In the most general context, users are the people who attempt to find information, or use a document, its surrogate, or representatives. This constitutes an enormous and broad class that for actual research would have to be very clearly defined in each study. Consider, would one expect the people in an academic library to have the same needs and interests as people in a public library or in a museum setting? In a high school setting, would one expect the information needs of the freshmen class to be the same as the senior? One of the issues becomes how to define the users and what about the users may be contributory to the study. Allen (1969) railed against using generic classifications such as "scientists" when the subjects studied were not research scientists but rather technologists, and the two groups do not exhibit the same communication behaviors. Information and communication behavior are areas of interest in user studies as a user's membership in a group may contribute to the manner in which he selects, investigates, or applies information resources. One area of bibliometric research is tracing the behaviors of certain users to determine how best to address their information requirements and how to enhance the information systems they may use. What comprises information behaviors is any activity involved in identifying and/or attempting to satisfy an information desire, interest, or need. It is thought that users might be classified by some characteristic, such as membership in an economic, age, educational discipline, or other type of group. If users could be grouped in this manner, it has been assumed that studying the information behavior of a sample of such a group could reveal how to better satisfy their needs.

A study to identify which information resources were most commonly consulted by science and engineering faculty might suggest other sources that might be fruitful to them. However, there is evidence that information seeking is limited to what is readily accessible or nearby (Lange, 1988). What is determined to be readily accessible is related to how critical the information is viewed, as in high steel construction workers, or pilots seeking weather details from federal weather sources, presumably because their lives depend upon accurate weather information (Schamber, 1991). Researchers have found that selection of sources for information is related to proximity or perceived ease of access. Experience with a source increased the likelihood of it being considered accessible, as did academic discipline and perceived utility. Travel distance required to access a source was a factor, with items physically at a distance considered less accessible than items in close proximity. On the electronic front, availability, location, and competition for access to a workstation was a consideration, as were personal experience with a resource, personal comfort, and a sense of expertise with a system (Abels, Liebscher and Denman, 1996). An earlier investigation examined information behaviors of how library and information professionals used e-mail distributed conferences for information seeking purposes. Problems with access were blamed for a low response rate, less than 6 percent, which also suggests that it might have been premature to explore a change of resource use based on the Internet. The respondents, however, indicated that the use of the e-conference systems did enhance information resources (Kovacs, Robinson and Dixon, 1995).

When undertaking user studies, one is trying to identify information behaviors, such as individuals' methods of seeking information, determining resources used, detecting what influences the behaviors and resources, as well as any constraints that might contribute to the behavior. The idea of information need has been a thorn for definition as well. User studies to explore behavior often have to confront the phrase "information need" as part of the user's makeup and part of the user's need to use information. Studies undertaken of users' behaviors and information needs are often performed as surveys, questionnaires, and interviews. There has been use of documentary sources such as circulation records, citation, and content analysis as well. Even simulation and role playing have been used (Rohde, 1986; Gorman, 1995).

As electronic resources have increased, more energy has been spent on evaluating how information seekers use electronic resources and what the impact is on professional or scholarly activity (Kaminer and Braunstein, 1998; Spink, Robins and Schamber, 1998). Allied to this is a growth in recognition of the importance of easy-to-use interfaces to information systems, whether online public access catalogs, vendored databases including DIALOG and LEXIS-NEXIS, or the Internet. So the tools and the requisite skills of the user have become part of the concerns of user studies. This also includes cognitive tools and analytical techniques employed in selecting or applying information (Wang and White, 1999).

Retrieval involves selection of information from a variety of sources. It also is dependent upon characteristics of both the seeker and potential source as well as all the handlers in between. How can a document be used if a potential user has no way to retrieve it? The user may not be able to frame the information request sufficiently to match the classification, cataloging, indexing, or other retrieval mechanism. Equally, the retrieval mechanism, the search agent, the classification, or subject identifier selection may not be appropriately reflective of the document. The user and the uses are special cases in each individual setting, with contributing complications from every turn, not to mention all the many instances of human interaction.

Finding fruitful and meaningful ways to examine "users" and "uses," objects of information, creation and content is still very much developmental and dramatically impacted by the new electronic resources with all the attendant complications. How to determine how users interact with traditional print materials has been a difficult and never satisfactorily resolved problem. Why is one document selected over another? Is it dictated by the user's sense of relevance to the information need, or is it ease of access? How can this be evaluated? Is a document used if it is moved from a shelf and left on a reshelfing cart? What is the measure of use? How is circulation indicative of use? Add to this electronic systems and wonder how user selection can be determined, measured, evaluated. Documents are no longer mere pieces of paper, or papyrus, or stone tablets, but more mediums than previously imagined. As many ways as there are to define a user, there are to define a use. Whether measuring either will yield any useful information is dependent upon the quality of the criteria invoked and the clarity of the definitions employed. These objects and representations of information and communication being the documentation and literature of our times, seeking to describe them by measurements and comparisons may yield new information, new theories, or the basis for prediction. Keep in mind, however, that describing things, even with quantitative measures, does not always lead to understanding or meaningful results.

## Summary

Bibliometrics may be used to measure and describe documents, surrogates, and even user behaviors. The act of description and measurement may reveal aspects of information units, which could be explored for other applications or interpretations. By measuring and evaluating features of information units, it may be possible to infer patterns of intellectual activity or interest. Tracing citations or co-citations may reveal research fronts, even disciplinary transformations. Applying measurement techniques does not ensure that there will be meaningful results, only that there may emerge new indicators of activity or areas to be reviewed. Bibliometrics opens a door and offers a path by which to examine components of the information and communication enigma.

# References

Abels, E. G., Liebscher, P. and Denman, D. W. 1996. Factors that Influence the Use of Electronic Networks by Science and Engineering Faculty at Small Institutions. Part I. Queries. *Journal of the American Society for Information Science* 47(2):146–158.

Allen, T. J. 1969. Information Needs and Users. *Annual Review of Information Science and Technology* pp. 3–29.

Bradford, S.C. 1948. *Documentation*. London: Crosby Lockwood.

Brookes, S.C. December 6, 1969. Bradford's Law and the Bibliography of Science. *Nature* 224 (5223):953–956.

Buckland, M. 1991. *Information and Information Systems*. New York, NY: Praeger.

Calhoun, C. C. 1995. Serials Citations and Holdings Correlation. *Library Resources & Technical Services* 39(1):53–76.

Campanario, J. M. 1996. Have Referees Rejected Some of the Most-Cited Articles of All Times? *Journal of the American Society for Information Science* 47(4):302-310.

Chen, H., Chung, Y., Ramsey, M. and Yang, C. C. 1998. A Smart Itsy Bitsy Spider for the Web. *Journal of the American Society for Information Science* 49(7):604–618.

Chowdhury, G. G. Summer 1999. Template Mining for Information Extraction from Digital Documents. *Library Trends* 48(1):182-208.

Dumas, T. 1993. In Focus: Using Citation Analysis and Subject Classification to Identify and Monitor Trends within a Discipline. In *Integrating Technologies: Converging Professions. Proceedings of the 56th Annual Meeting of the American Society for Information Science, October 24–28, Columbus, OH* 30:135–150.

Fayyad, U. 1996. Data Mining and Knowledge Discovery: Making Sense Out of Data. *IEEE Expert* 11(5):20–25.

Fayyad, U., Piatetsky-Shapiro, G., and Smyth, P. 1996. From Data Mining to Knowledge Discovery in Databases. *Ai Magazine* 17(3):37–54.

Gorman, P. N. 1995. Information Needs of Physicians. *Journal of the American Society for Information Science* 46(10):729–736.

Kaminer, N. and Braunstein, Y. M. 1998. Bibliometric Analysis of the Impact of Internet Use on Scholarly Productivity. *Journal of the American Society for Information Science* 49(8):720–730.

Kovacs, D. K, Robinson, K. L. and Dixon, J. 1995. Scholarly E-Conference on the Academic Networks: How Library and Information Science Professionals Use Them. *Journal of the American Society for Information Science* 46(4):244–253.

Lange, J. M. 1987/1988. Public Library Users, Nonusers, and Type of Library Use. *Public Library Quarterly* 8, 1/2:49–67.

Lewis, D. D. and Jones, K. S. 1996. Natural Language Processing for Information Retrieval. *Communications of the ACM* 39(1):92–101.

Lokta, A.J. 1926. The Frequency Distribution of Scientific Productivity. *Journal of the Washington Academy of Science,* 16(12):317–323.

Losee, R. M. and Haas, S. W. 1995. Sublanguage Terms: Dictionaries, Usage, and Automatic Classification. *Journal of the American Society for Information Science* 46(7): 519–529.

Pao, M. L. 1989. *Concepts of Information Retrieval.* Englewood, CO: Libraries Unlimited.

Rohde, N. F. 1986. Information Needs. *Advances in Librarianship* 14:49–73.

Schamber, L. 1991. User's Criteria for Evaluation in Multimedia Information Seeking and Use Situations. Unpublished Doctoral Dissertation. Syracuse University.

Spink, A., Robins, D., and Schamber, L. 1998. Use of Scholarly Book Reviews: Implications for Electronic Publishing and Scholarly Communication. *Journal of the American Society for Information Science* 49(4):364–374.

Taylor, A. G. 1999. *The Organization of Information.* Englewood, CO: Libraries Unlimited.

Tsay, M-Y. 1998. Library Journal Use and Citation Half-Life in Medical Science. *Journal of the American Society for Information Science* 49(14):1283–1292.

van der Wurff, B. March 1997. Out of Particles. Centre for Science and Technology Studies (CWTS). [online, April 1999] available: http://sahara.fsw.leidenuniv.nl/cwts/noframes/cernintr.html

Vickery, B. C. and Vickery, A. 1987. *Information Science in Theory and Practice.* London, UK: Butterworth.

Wang, P. and White, M. D. 1999. A Cognitive Model of Document Use during a Research Project. Study II. Decisions at the Reading and Citing Stage. *Journal of the American Society for Information Science* 46(4):244–253.

White, H. D. and McCain, K. W. 1989. Bibliometrics. In M. E. Williams, (Ed.). *Annual Review of Information Science and Technology* 24:119–186.

Wiebe, J., Hirst, G. and Horton, D. 1996. Language Use in Context. *Communications of the ACM* 39(1):102–111.

# Chapter 6

# Information Economics

## Introduction

Traditionally, information economics has focused on information products and processes, evaluating the efficiency of information transfer systems as processes of input, output, and added value or scrutinizing an economic transaction to ascertain equity (King, Roderer and Olsen, 1983). Another view of information economics depicts the impetus of information and its related technology as affecting economic, social, political, and cultural constructs the world over, not just within the framework of processes and products but as symptomatic of a cycle of information and knowledge growth (Castells, 1993; Tapscott, 1996). To discuss information economics, there are several concepts that require examination. First, information has dramatic economic implications. This is the information age, or information economy, with stakeholders, participants with something to risk, not entirely unlike other economic periods. Second, there are characteristics of economics that are important in the discussion of the information age, such as resources and uncertainty. Third, concerns about the assignment of value and assessment of cost are central to information economics. Fourth, and last here, though not last in the larger discipline, the combination of economics and information significantly impact decision making in organizations and hence organizational information behaviors. This section will address each of the first two components at a rudimentary level, while the third and fourth area will be covered in separate chapters. An explanation of the use of models as used in a variety of disciplines will supplement this chapter and provide foundation for posing some information and economic models. The rationale for venturing into this arena in an introductory text is simply that the concepts of economics pertinent to information and the area of information economics will only continue to grow and acquire more importance to the information professions. Accepting this as the case is the first step in recognizing where the information professions may lead.

## Economics

Economics in the broadest sense may be considered the activities undertaken to provide for the satisfaction of desires. As such, the study of economics has created theories and models to explain the activities, to examine the functions and interactions, and to delineate the character of economic systems. Economic systems are structures, or series of structures, through which interactions occur, which contribute to the satisfaction of desires (Redman and Redman, 1981). In general, economics is based on two related activities, production and consumption; production is the creation of items to be consumed and consumption is the obtaining, typically through purchase or barter of the items produced. However, consumption may also refer to the use of resources. Resources are the materials—land, labor, and capital—that are used in production. There is a cycle implied in these activities, which is rooted in resources. Economics as a study is interested in "principles governing the allocation of scarce means among competing ends when the objectives of the allocation are to maximize the attainment of those ends" (p. 1). Scarce means are resources. In economics, resources are considered scarce "because they are limited, all uses cannot be satisfied at the same time" (p. 1). There are only so many dollars in a budget, only so much space in a building, only so much land available to grow certain crops. All of these could be considered scarce resources because they are limited in availability and can be used for only one action at a time. Certain resources, such as air, stand outside of this assertion since air is not considered scarce and is therefore considered to have a zero value in economics. However, other thoughts in the area of resources have turned up a new variant, information.

Information may be considered a resource, albeit an unusual one, because it is not scarce in the traditional sense. Information can be applied in more than one situation, is not readily containable, is easily transported, and exhibits characteristics that are not within the traditional model of resources. Information can be compressed and summarized. Information can be used in place of other types of resources, robots working on factory lines instead of people is one example of information replacing labor (Cleveland, 1982). Further, information in certain cases can be considered a commodity, an article of trade, an item for consumption (Cleveland; Schiller, 1988). Innovations in technology, specifically electronics, telecommunications, computer and related information system components, have influenced the manner in which human beings undertake both economic and social activities. The resulting changes have modified the economic structures previously accepted and are indicative of significant and continued transformations on a global scale for some time to come. The traditional basis of economics, as defined above, rooted in production and consumption based upon resource scarcity, demand, supply, and exchange has become more complex as the attributes of information and its technologies become more integrated into the economy (Cleveland; Castells, 1993).

## The Information Economy

It has long been established that information and its related industries and activities are critical expanding economic components of the United States' and the global economy (Black and Marchand, 1982; Carnoy, Castells, Cohen and Cardoso, 1993; Cleveland, 1982; Cooper, 1983; Lamberton, 1984; Lanvin, 1995; Porter and Millar 1985; Robinson, 1986; Rubin and Sapp, 1981). Researchers around the world have concluded that information and its industries are economic entities with significant current and future prospective for economic growth and power (Goodman, 1987; Lanvin, 1995; Nora and Minc, 1980). Over the last three decades it has become evident that economic growth in traditional sectors, such as agriculture, manufacturing, and trade, is dramatically and intrinsically bound to the capacity to use information and its technologies competitively. Improved information resources such as faster and more accurate weather forecasting, more detailed soil analysis, new insight into erosion control, stock feed formulation, and more efficient farm machinery contribute enormously to the agricultural productivity of the United States. National Agricultural Statistics Services (NASS) on February 8, 1999, released a Year 2000 Readiness report that indicates 32 percent of farmers in the United States are using computerized systems. The automated farm systems in use included recordkeeping, irrigation, feeding systems, storage systems for grain, vegetable or produce, milking machines, milk storage, heating, cooling and ventilation for livestock, and global positioning systems (online, 1999). Manufacturing and industry use information technology to improve timeline estimates on projects and to enhance competitiveness by saving money for customers by meeting or beating deadlines (Villano, 1999). Use of better gathering and implementation of information from point of sale by large retailers improves product purchasing, helps maintain balanced inventory, identifies regional product preferences and customer profiles, and produces real savings by having the appropriate products in the right places in the correct quantities. This information flow leads to greater customization of factory orders to serve particular retailers or wholesalers. In turn, this enables better factory floor project management and market sensitive production. All of these are improved supply chain practices that save time and money by having production activities in sync with demand, as well as putting materials in regions where they are known to be marketable (Caldwell and Violino, 1999; Engler, 1999; Stein and Sweat, 1998). The actual enterprises involved in the creation, accumulation, application, and manipulation of information, as well as its related technologies and related offspring, are actually economically productive in ways not previously recognized (Castells, 1993).

Just as there was a significant number of laborers working in the agricultural sector who shifted to the industrial sector and its factories in the nineteenth and early portion of the twentieth century, in the second half of the twentieth century labor has shifted from agriculture and factories into the service, knowledge, or information sector. This movement into offices, sometimes into virtual ones, and a variety of service positions has been the result of changing technology, especially in the area of information exchange, telecommunications, and automation. The manner in which factories operate has been changed by automation, and the management of those facilities has been modified by information exchange and telecommunications. Decisions are based on information from agents in distant places and are no longer restricted by limited communication facilities (Castells, 1993). Information that provides insight into the corporate conduct influences the value of stocks, managerial portfolios, and public image. The underlying infrastructures of governments and economies are being impacted as a result of increasing communications potential, larger and more diverse markets (Bar, 1995; Garcia, 1995; Nicolaidis, 1995). Providing access to the new multiple layers of information has weighed upon the budgets of libraries and educational and research organizations (Henderson, 1999). New technology spawns new opportunities, new challenges, and more new technology.

The information economy has the potential and impetus to dramatically change the globe. This is not to suggest that it is an evenly distributed or balanced phenomena, because it is not. In the United States there are distinct economic borders that separate people into technology haves and have-nots. As recently as 1997, the distribution of United States households owning computers was only 35 percent. These were skewed toward higher ownership based upon level of education, 65.6 percent of owners had attended graduate school, 56.2 percent were college graduates, and 22.5 percent were high school graduates. Ethnically, of the 35 percent owning computers, 48 percent were Asian, 35 percent were white and 17 percent were black (Monthly Labor Review, online, 1999). There are people and nations with limited access to the fiscal resources required to support a high-tech economy. Despite media hype, there are still large portions of the globe with serious infrastructure concerns that limit or impact technological access, such as poor transportation systems for materials or electronics; insufficient educational tools to promote technological development; and a dozen other more pressing human needs like food, housing, and safety. There are also serious cultural implications as the information age and economy indiscriminately disseminate the advertising and cultural icons of the nations with sophisticated broadcast systems, radio, television, satellite, and Internet (Haywood, 1995). This is not to diminish the importance of the information economy but to remind us that there are positive and negative aspects to this creature, and it will have far reaching economic and social effects that should not be overlooked.

*Stakeholders*

Ultimately, the information age has the potential to affect everyone on the planet in some way and thereby in the broadest sense, it will make everyone a stakeholder. In a smaller sense, the technological information evolution is certainly impacting participants in both developed nations and emerging economies. Direct stakeholders range from the telecommunications industries, which may optionally hold the most sway over future development, along with the computer hardware and software manufacturers; the industrial sector, now dependent upon automation and information for efficiency and the appearance of cost savings; the research industry in any field, bound to the past and the future by the information technology and the impact of its economies; governments of all levels; and people, those who have access to information resources and the information economy and those who do not yet, and might not ever. The stakeholders all have something to gain or to lose related to their willingness and their current ability to risk. Their abilities are based on what their economic resources are, what fiscal or fiscally comparable things they have to invest, and how well they can move that investment into growth, or at least stability.

Corporations, small businesses, nonprofits, educational, and governmental bodies are all stakeholders. To fully explore the notion of stakeholders, consider a business that produces computer chips. If their research and development department fails to keep current with changing technology, changing design methods, or lacks creativity, the product will become obsolete within eighteen months. If the product is considered obsolete, fewer products will be purchased; if this cycle goes too far, the business will fail. Everyone who worked for the business is out of work, everyone who relied on those workers buying goods from them—e.g., restaurants, car dealers, grocery stores—suffers a loss of income. If there is not a resolution, at least partial, a cycle of economic downturn occurs and all the stakeholders become very apparent, because everyone who is affected is a stakeholder. The level of stakeholders' involvement may vary. This is a large view of stakeholders, more often a smaller view is easier to comprehend. In the smaller view, the backers and workers of business and their direct contacts would be the stakeholders.

## Resources

Traditional economic resources are "means of supplying what is needed" (Allen, 1984, p. 636), and these resources are considered limited, which contributes to a value system for exchange of resources. Silver is a natural resource, an ore, with limited availability in nature and enormous usefulness in society. It is a component of a variety of medical, photographic, and pharmaceutical materials, as well as being treasured as a precious metal. This resource has a physical, tangible character, which is also finite; it is possible to extract all of the useable silver ore from the earth. When that happens the value of the mined ore, as well as the value of the objects containing this ore, will increase as the silver becomes scarcer. Alternatively, finding resources to replace silver in critical products would decrease the demand and possibly prevent an ore crisis. One of the ways to determine whether there are alternatives for silver in various processes and products for which it is used requires research into the aspects of the ore and its handling that makes it useful. Such research involves significant investigation of the ore, its properties, its uses, and any related metals or materials that might be used as substitutes.

Modern information technologies, computer analysis systems, measurement devices, databases, chemical analysis methods, and information-based tools provide avenues for the exploration of alternatives to tangible scarce resources. Information is a resource in that it contributes to satisfying needs and desires, but it is very different in most other aspects. Tangible, physical resources, such as ore, lumber, machines, equipment, land, minerals, gems, are limited as in scarce; they can be depleted and diminished, a truck can be in only one place at a time and can be used for one activity at a time, and these tangible things cannot be held by more than one person at a time. These are not the characteristics of information. According to Cleveland (1982) information is expandable, that is, all the information is never fully acquired, information grows, it compounds upon itself and is added to over time; it is not scarce. (However, the volume of information available can actually make useable information nearly inaccessible, but this is not entirely the same as being totally depleted as an ore might become.) Just as information is expandable, it is also compressible, its formats can be modified, can be distilled, abstracted, summarized, as into a formula. There will be some loss of information with such compression. It is not possible to compress a truck, or an ore, in the same manner.

The application of information can be used to substitute for resources, such as new information about silver alternatives, or substituting automation for human labor. Information may be transported at the speed of light. Information is diffusive, it spreads, it changes, it has been the greatest threat to oppressive governments. Information can be conveyed via a commercial, a photograph, a body language expression, or hidden in the words of a novel or a newspaper. Information is shareable, unlike tangible goods. If someone is given a ring, the giver no longer has the ring, only the receiver; if someone is given an idea, both the giver and receiver have the idea. Additionally, the receiver may be able to improve upon the idea, expand it, find a new application for it. These differences make information a unique resource, which can and does modify how we function with both tangible and intangible resources and virtually every aspect of our economic and cultural endeavors (Cleveland, 1982).

## Uncertainty

The concept of uncertainty is integral across the spectrum of economic theories, especially in the areas of decision making, organizational theory, theory of finance, risk aversion (insurance theory), game theory, price theory and even equilibrium theory (McCall, 1982). The works of Kenneth J. Arrow, J. Marschak and R. Radner in the description and application of the notions of uncertainty have had profound effects on the field of economics. Indeed, the work of these individuals did much to bring the concept of uncertainty into virtually all areas of economic study (McCall; Heller, Starr and Starretti, 1986).

What is uncertainty? What is its role in information economics? Arrow defined information as "the negative measure of uncertainty" (Arrow, 1984). Stated alternatively, lack of information is the measure of uncertainty. As Arrow points out, while there are theoretical quantifications for uncertainty—for use in mathematical modeling of economics activities primarily, such as decision making—there is no well-established quantitative measure for information. Arrow concedes, however, that while Shannon's measure of information does not provide a value for information, it may be applicable in determining the cost of acquisition of information. Despite the lack of measures applicable to information, the concept of uncertainty is simply the lack of information that might be pertinent to the economic activity at hand.

The concept of uncertainty is usually represented by applications of probabilities, that is, the likelihood of x condition, or outcome occurring. We must consider in this that for the sake of analysis and discussion, economists have typically chosen to use models and methods that permit them to obtain a result, regardless of the actual parameters of the issue under study. Arrow emphasizes this in his discussion of Decision Theory. "There is no point in posing a problem for which we cannot find the solution, so we tend to modify our formulation of the problem in order to make it practical" (1984, p. 56). This usually means eliminating those aspects of a situation from a model that are difficult to measure or to evaluate. This view strengthens the application of uncertainty as a probability function as it permits economists, and those engaged in economic decision making, to establish artificial parameters to the probability. These parameters are easily viewed through Teams and Game Theory, that is, as rules to the game (Phlips, 1982).

In various situations, what the information is that might reduce uncertainty is also an issue of uncertainty and is as critical as the information itself (Arrow; Green and Laffont, 1986; Rothschild, 1986). Consider uncertainty about game rules or the lack of adequate definition of the parameters. If "rules include the set of payoffs, the set of strategies and the number of players," then an example is "An auction in which the bidders do not know what value the other bidders attach to the auctioned object..."; this means that the "players do not know each others' payoffs" (Phlips, p. 9). This problem of uncertainty about parameters is handled by redefinition of the game so that each player knows the possibility of a result, in this case the payoff parameter "that is uncertain" (p. 9).

Two inferences can be drawn from the discussion so far. First, it is necessary for modeling and analytical reasons to establish artificial parameters to cope with uncertainty. Second, establishing such artificial parameters may contribute to uncertainty. By substituting additional probabilistic properties for information, the information available to reduce uncertainty may be diminished. The underlying assumption that permits multiple substitution of probabilities for information is that each of the players is now operating from the same substitutions, thereby replacing not only missing information (the quality of uncertainty) but also equalizing the playing field in submission to equilibrium theory (Newman, 1983).

Consider, there are four card players using a single fifty-two card deck, and the object of the game is to obtain groups of four matching cards, regardless of suit. Each play may first draw five cards, then after that each player may draw one card and keep it or return it to the deck, face down. First, all four players are aware that there are twenty cards in hand, which means there are only thirty-two cards in the deck. There are thirteen possible sets of four cards. This information provides each player with the possibility of pulling the cards needed from the deck as they play. If cards are returned to the deck face down, then each player, as he or she takes a turn, learns a new card, gains information, while the other three players do not; however, the balance of uncertainty is maintained because each of the three players also gains card knowledge in the process of their turns. The balance is slightly changed if the returned card is returned face up, as then all the players have the same information at the same time about the new card, but uncertainty remains because each player still holds his or her own unique cards, which the other players do not know about. Over the course of the game as more cards are revealed, uncertainty will decrease. Depending on the rules of the game and the deck, the players can devise ways to estimate the tolerable level of risk taking to achieve a desired outcome. When rules are unclear, or circumstances can be modified without all the players being aware of the changes, then information iniquity occurs and the playing field is not level.

Information economics is concerned with the effects that information (uncertainty reduction) or the lack of information (uncertainty) can generate (Arrow, 1984). Essentially, information economics attempts to take into account the variations created by the presence, absence, extent, and distribution of information in economic structures. Some of the characteristics of information (Cleveland, 1982), such as its expandability, work to undermine equilibrium or balance. For example, in the redefinition of the game, applying agreed upon probabilities in substitution for areas of uncertainty could actually provide information for one of the players. When card players agree that one-eyed jacks will be wild cards, they are substituting probabilities, increasing the likelihood of more wild cards, which increases uncertainty (Myerson, 1986). The game returns to a state of disequilibrium caused by an imbalance in uncertainty distribution, which is a violation of the validity of the probability substitutions for the uncertainty variant.

The tradition of research in uncertainty as a component of information economics continues to adhere to the use of the models where uncertainty is replaced by probabilistic structures. The research covers the areas of game theory, decision making, organizational theory, risk aversion (insurance theory), and finance theory, among many others. Newer works continue to apply the traditional models of uncertainty, as well as other traditional models of economics, to issues of cost consideration in information production, information evaluation, planning and information, and cost-benefits analysis of information, to name a few (King, Roderer and Olsen, 1983). Until new models or approaches are devised, the replacement of uncertainty variants with probabilistic structures will continue. This is not necessarily irrational, since even these models provide information about uncertainty aspects by virtue of their failings (Arrow, 1984).

## Models

### Introduction

Seeking to better understand the world around us, we attempt to create imitations of our world, of circumstances, systems, organisms, ourselves, and our societies. From these imitations, which are usually more simplistic representations of our perceptions, we attempt to extrapolate further information about the world. This imitation is not limited to attempts to duplicate or even simulate an arena of study, rather, it includes attempts to apply forms and imagination to an arena that is not typically viewed in the light of the imitative form we may choose. The application of Shannon and Weaver's (1949) theory of information transfer, a statistically based examination of the flow of electronic signals and noise in a telecommunication structure, to the more general and nonelectronic transfer of information among individuals would be such a case (Wilkin, 1977). The initial intention of their work was to find ways to estimate the amount of signal necessary to overcome unintended signals in conducting channels to ensure clarity of communication. This notion was seized upon in other fields as the basis for the sender-channel-receiver model considered essential to understanding human communication and information behavior.

The imitations are referred to as models. Models have been used by physical scientists for centuries as ways of representing the world, even the universe, while attempting to use the models as a means of explaining and understanding phenomena. Admittedly many models were flawed, limited at their inception by the limitations of the era and the men who envisioned them. Aristotle's and Ptolemy's geocentric system, which placed the Earth as the center of the universe, are classical flawed models yet were held as truth for centuries. Even when Copernicus set forth a new model with the Sun as the center of the universe, his model demanded planetary motion be perfectly circular. Keeler ultimately resolved some of the contradictions that circular planetary motion demonstrated, but longingly persisted in modeling the universe on a geometry model of nested polyhedrons. Many of the models that were proposed were heavily influenced by the political and religious climates of the time. Even Keeler was seeking some spiritual force in the motion of the planets, some higher order of mystical comprehension of the unknown (Boorstin, 1983). Those models, though far short of what is now understood, led ultimately to knowledge today.

Social sciences have lagged behind in modeling. Many of the models used in the physical sciences are mathematically based. It has taken considerable time and debate to bring mathematical structures into the social sciences. Moreover, it has taken time to recognize that modeling need not be entirely math-based; models may be exploratory structures that encourage inquiry and speculation. Models do not have to be static, nor are models the solution to issues, but rather a method for examining issues.

The intent of this section is to look at models, and issues surrounding models, relative to the social sciences. This section will be a brief exploration of model history, with some applications of models to issues in the library and information field. Models hold tremendous potential as diagnostic and test tools in the practical and theoretical work of library and information science.

## *Debating Models in Social Science*

In 1967, a symposium on the Process of Model-Building in the Behavioral Sciences was conducted at Ohio State University. The symposium was to discuss the process of model building and as such had to engage in a certain amount of definition. The underlying premise that undefined models are often accepted without explanation as accurate approaches to problems was a serious topic of concern. The participants attempted to discourse upon the activities and criteria that should be undertaken in model building. What ensued was an enlightening collection of diverse views that underlines the continuing conflict about the construction and role of models.

Stogdill (1970) considered models to be the same as theories, only shorter lived. Stogdill suggested that models should be based in scientific method, problems conceptualized logically and empirically. Moreover, he saw model building as a creative process that is not clearly understood. Luce (1970) described models as atheoritic, that is, methods for testing isolated properties of a theory, which may not be adequately representative of the theory. Atheoritic models are employed as a mechanism for exploring subsets of a theory; the results may or may not be expandable beyond the original subset. Ashby (1970) contended that models are constructs devised to approximate a portion of a real system, for the purpose of convenience and the reduction of information that is inherent in the creation of the artifice. For the purposes of investigation, Ashby accepted models as useful and legitimate tools if scientific methods of analysis appropriate to the problem under study were applied. In the framework of appropriate scientific analysis, Ashby perceived the value of a model as directly related to its ability to reflect the real world. The strength of that reflection being demonstrated via the model's ability to be tested and its trueness to the system being modeled. Morris (1970) submitted that models need not be part of reality but rather distinct from reality. The abstract model is developed into a state that reflects reality through a process of testing whether the model is adequately descriptive of the problem and through the ability to treat the model as a deductive tool. Morris' notion of models suggested the use of analogy drawn from established precepts. Morris further indicated that while fields such as engineering have many prior models to work from, the emerging sciences do not. C. West Churchman took exception to all the above characterizations of models. He questioned whether it was appropriate to model reality, since the model could only be a subset and could not take into account "the real world which is very complex and largely unknown" (1970, p. 135). Yet, as Churchman pointed out, people want to draw from this unknown to create an artifice by which to study the unknown. Churchman contended that reality should be "all the relevant challenges of the model" (p. 137), and he quotes E. A. Singer's "Reality is the repository of all unanswered questions." Churchman proposed that models are built in direct response to questions and are the result of an organized trial and error system attempting to respond to a question.

A synthesis of all of these opinions offers the best available description of models. Models are investigative tools. The reliability, acceptability, and validity of the results of the application of these tools should be suspect as we are investigating unknowns from various perspectives. At the same time, the usefulness and creative stimulation that models offer should not be underestimated. Models that adhere to scientific methodology based on accepted scientific theories and laws might, from a scientific point of view, be considered superior to models composed without proper foundation in the known. However, if models were limited to the known, there would be little point to using them at all (Churchman, 1970). It is in exploration that models are useful, but models are merely tools and do not prove nor disprove. It is essential to be aware of the shortcomings and appropriate application of these tools whether they be founded in fact or fiction, or a mixture of both.

### Applying Models

Models do not necessarily need to spring from the known, but they should be designed and applied with some rigor to secure their usefulness. This can be extremely difficult. The application of models can be divided between those that are testable, in the scientific sense, and those that are not. John Maynard Smith (1982) contrasted simple models used for creative impetus or investigation versus models dealing with critical areas that might directly affect lives. Modeling the breakdown of a nuclear reactor demands more attention to detail and reality then modeling a Web engine information exchange. In applying various game theory models to evolutionary behaviors, Smith took great pains to detail the structure of the models: the assumptions, strategies and limitations, which the design of the model and his applications of them imposed. The use of game theory models was an opportunity to explore a problem from a different view, basically two models are better than one. But this conclusion can only be drawn because of prior analysis that was undertaken before bringing in the game theory model. Smith used the models as methods of testing and attempting to predict certain outcomes, but he did not use the models as the definitive result, rather as a path to inquiry. Specific shortcomings of a model should be clarified at the outset to ensure there is no confusion about the expectations and the potential extrapolations of the results. For example, applying game theory models to biological systems would entail specifying how the model cannot work, and what assumptions or implied circumstances are involved. By stating the assumptions and design of the models Smith proposed to employ in his inquiry, he gave those who would study his work a method for evaluating, criticizing, and replicating, or even modifying his models with new information. The foundations of modern science rely upon such capacities. That Smith managed to arrange his models with such formality relies upon an aspect of models that Ashby (1970) pointed out: models allow for the reduction of information. A model need not encompass all the complexities of the phenomenon it represents; rather the model permits the extraction of parts for examination. As long as the fact that the model is not a total representation of the phenomenon is recognized, fruitful exploration may result. It is when the model is supposed or reported to be fully representative in every way of the phenomenon under consideration, that grave pseudo-information is produced.

## Models and Information

Models are employed in a variety of settings concerned with information. Information retrieval models based on computer-implemented retrieval tend to be categorized as traditional or interactive. The traditional model, the initial evolution of computer retrieval, resulted from the limitations of the machine. Retrieval activities were based on primitive matching algorithms dependent upon the quality of the record surrogate and the capacity of the system to manipulate the records. This yielded results that were often completely disconnected from the actual search interest. Studying this retrieval scenario led to recognition that relevance was an important but overlooked (or under computed) aspect of successful retrieval (Spink, 1997). Users of systems such as DIALOG developed techniques to improve the relevance of retrieval by progressively refining their searches. This weighing of results, seeking after more items that are similar to the ones selected for the second run, when put into a machine algorithm produced an automatic retrieval system. This is a relevance feedback method and was strongly based upon what the user deemed as relevant. Variations of this model continue to this day.

A newer model is developing that allows for interactive feedback on a variety of measures; preliminary research with this approach suggests important advantages. Multiple types of interactive feedback may significantly improve search results. It is evident that the cognitive involvement in the interactive model provides more feedback opportunities than a single automatic relevance conducted through direct programming (Spink, 1997). By creating a system upon which to test the retrieval process, a model produces results that can be explored, using as many configurations as the researcher can imagine and justify.

Case study models are another tactic for examining issues. A common case study model usually involves reference desk questions or difficult patron queries. Aluri (1993) points out that the reference setting is actually a single element in a much larger system and may be impacted by a list of variables, ranging from physical environment to conflicting philosophies and practices. To model a reference interview, or to construct a method for evaluating reference work, would entail accounting for all the variables and how they interact with the ability of the reference personnel to perform. Setting a scene with various scripts to work out the best way to handle a situation could be a powerful model. It is also possible to extend these types of models by using actually documented occurrences and reenacting them to determine if an alternative solution could have changed the result. It is also a way to explore all the possible options for situations before they come to pass; this could provide important input to policy design. Recognizing the complexity of a situation may be the primary result of attempting to devise a testable model.

### Models in an Economics Context

Modeling may be adventurous and creative but these limitations imposed on the model must be clear, or extrapolations that lead to confusion are created. One such case would be Harlan Cleveland's (1982) discussion of information as a resource in an economic sense. In economics, resources are considered scarce "because they are limited, all uses cannot be satisfied at the same time" (Redman and Redman, 1981, p. 1). Certain resources, such as air, stand outside of this assertion since air is not considered scarce and is therefore considered to have a zero value in economics. According to Cleveland, information may be considered a resource, albeit an unusual one, because it is not scarce in the traditional sense; it can be applied in more than one situation, is not readily containable, and exhibits characteristics which are not within the traditional model of resources. Further, information in certain cases can be considered a commodity, an article of trade, an item for consumption (Cleveland; Schiller, 1988). How information is evaluated in economics may depend upon which economic approach is applied. Hence, a model must be clarified to be fully explored. But to clarify the model, a further venture into economics is required.

There are two primary approaches to economics, one of these, macroeconomics, concerns itself with studying the components of a system as a whole, or an average, rather than the individual parts. Macroeconomics tries to examine and investigate the relationships and interactions among these aggregate entities (Redman and Redman, 1981).

For example, government policies concerned with large groups, such as policies governing the telecommunications industry, would be a macroeconomic topic. Essentially, macroeconomics considers the larger economic system by focusing on national economics, or global economics, or on entire industries in collective. The interrelationships of the various components of the economy are critical to the macro view. Macroeconomic models are built to imitate the larger economy and the relationships among the components that construct the economy.

Another approach is microeconomic, the study "of the individual firm and industry" (Redman and Redman, 1981, p. 7). It examines wages, price, and income in a particular firm or unit setting. Microeconomics is concerned with the specifics of the individual units that comprise the economy. The study of the microeconomics approaches economic analysis through examination of the firm or the market, outside of the confines of the larger economy (Redman and Redman).

Whether from a macroeconomic view or from a microeconomic view, working with models affects the perspective of analysis; the models are predominately the same, merely adjusted to reflect the larger or smaller extrapolation that will be generated. Both approaches use idealized, generalized, abstracted perfect structure models that are supposed to be representative of the economic entity under study. Information from a general macroeconomic view would be a national policy issue, a resource, and potentially an interrelationship in the formulation of macro outcome. In a microeconomic view, information may be a resource or a commodity, and as the alternative to uncertainty, might be a critical feature of a micro analysis. However, with few exceptions, information as a component of the models in macro or micro economics is typically treated as a noncontributor, and information's negative, which is uncertainty, is represented merely as an unknown value that is carried around in the equations (Bickner, 1983; Chick, 1983).

Many of the economic models that have been applied to information do not account for the dynamic nature of information as outlined by Cleveland (1982) and Arrow (1984). In particular, the microeconomic version of models is too limited in scope to account for the diverse and almost unpredictable qualities of information. Information does not act in a vacuum or even in a frozen time frame. Information is not necessarily limited to the firm or to the market and as such may have effects outside of the model; these may ultimately rebound upon the model. These assertions about economic models are not new and are typically overlooked in general, but with the emerging potential of information, it is no longer acceptable to apply models that ignore primary aspects of information and therefore could dramatically affect the outcome of a model application. Macroeconomic versions of models are often just as artificial as the micro versions, but the nature of the approach involves taking more variables into consideration and therefore yields more dynamic results.

The limitations of the models from either micro or macro economics are rarely if ever stated when applying them. This omission leads to misunderstandings when other fields, such as the information fields, attempt to employ the models from economics. In applying game theory models to biology, Smith (1982) was extremely cautious to outline the shortcomings of both game theory and the impact that it could have on examining a biological system from that model viewpoint. No confusion was allowed to enter into the discourse via omission. As indicated above, much confusion has been allowed to enter into areas employing economics models. Indeed, as already stated, models are used to reduce the information that needs examination, or even act in nonrepresentative fashion, but the reduction of points, the variance from representation, the limitations and resulting possible pitfalls must be identified. Further, certain characteristics essential to the problem being modeled should not be omitted. As Morris (1970) suggested, a model must be adequately descriptive to the problem it is applied to, or the resulting assumptions could be completely false. A determination of the descriptive qualities of the problem depends upon a careful analysis of the problem prior to any attempt to simulate it.

A case where the application of a model may suggest misleading conclusions would be the application of the Cobb-Douglas production model to public libraries (Hayes, 1979). The Cobb-Douglas model deals with production as a function of capital and labor. It operates on "production per employee" and "capital investment per employee"; both of these are generally considered in a strictly quantitatively measurable environment such as an automobile factory, where each part and each product can be assigned costs in both material and labor. The application of the model could be viewed as an adventurous investigation into its applicability to libraries. Depending upon how it was applied, it might have some illustrative power, but to equate a library system to a primary production system would require significant clarification of all the parameters and very careful evaluation.

The application of the Cobb-Douglas model might be creative and may in time, with extended foundation, be a useful model to modify for use in library management settings. The problem, however, requires further analysis and definition before we should go into such a model. Employing mathematical models requires clearly defining the sources of the numbers, as well as being certain of the appropriate interpretation of any resulting statistics.

Economic models can be applied with reasonable success to the information fields. Lancaster's (1971) work in cost-effectiveness explains how such an analysis can be undertaken. Like Smith's (1982) carefully documented work, Lancaster clearly establishes the path that must be traveled and the special circumstances that must be considered. He specifically identified what the sources of cost are and supports that identification with examples. Cost-effectiveness is defined with the variables identified and the role of a cost-benefit model identified. Additionally, the basic steps involved in the analysis are clearly stated and further explained. Lancaster actually creates a model that could be applied to information fields via his careful explanation of how to view the components of a cost-effectiveness model with information fields in mind.

## Models Summary

Despite diversity of opinions about models, they have been used throughout human history as investigative tools. When models are constructed with attention to classical scientific method, as recommended by Ashby (1970) and Stogdill (1970), and demonstrated by Smith (1982) and Lancaster (1971), they can be employed in hypothesis testing and data gathering. Methodically constructed models could be utilized in all fields of inquiry as long as there is a method to the structure. The method should be in the result of a comprehensive analysis, within the limitations of that analysis. The model may lead the investigator into further analysis or down a garden path, but the foundation model must be clearly defined regardless of its source derivation. What is key to Lancaster's work, to Smith's work, and to the work of many other successful modelers is the comprehension that models are not the "solve-all." Models are investigative tools, with limitations that must be identified and ultimately dealt with, within the framework of the problem being modeled.

## Summary

Economics as a study is complex, made more so when considered with information as a component. Information economics will evolve as a different creature than previous economic forms because of the potential for cross-pollination on all fronts of activity. Aspects of information and its contrary uncertainty will have to be addressed in a more specific manner rather than having the possible outcomes ignored. The implications of information economics to all spheres, social, political, and financial, are tremendous and unpredictable, because the transformation of information into an evolving resource, difficult to model or to control, suggests that we will not be able to rely on previous systems of integrating the notions of information into economic constructs.

## References

Allen, R. E., (Ed.). 1984. *The Pocket Oxford Dictionary of Current English.* 7th Ed. New York, NY: Oxford University Press.

Aluri, R. 1993. Improving Reference Service: The Case for Using Continuous Quality Improvement Method. *RQ* 33(2):220–236.

Arrow, K. J. 1984. *Collected Papers of Kenneth J. Arrow: The Economics of Information,* vol. 4. Cambridge, MA: Belknap Press of Harvard University Press.

Ashby, W. R. 1970. Analysis of the System to Be Modeled. In *The Process of Model Building in the Behavioral Sciences* pp. 94–114. Ohio State University Press.

Bar, F. 1995. Information Infrastructure and the Transformation of Manufacturing. In W. J. Drake, (Ed.) *The New Information Infrastructure: Strategies for United States Policy* pp. 55–74. New York, NY: The Twentieth Century Fund Press.

Bickner, R. E. 1983. Concepts of Economic Cost. In D. W. King, N. K. Roderer and H. A. Olsen, (Eds.) *Key Papers in the Economics of Information* pp. 10–49. White Plains, NY: Knowledge Industry Publications.

Black, S.H. and Marchand, D. A. 1982. Assessing the Value of Information in Organizations: A Challenge for the 1980's, *The Information Society* 1(3):191–225.

Boorstin, D. J. 1983. *The Discovers*. New York, NY: Random House.

Caldwell, B. and Violino, B. March 1, 1999. Hyper-Efficient Companies. *Information-Week*. Issue 728:40–51.

Carnoy, M., Castells, M., Cohen, S. S. and Cardoso, F. H. 1993. *The New Global Economy in the Information Age: Reflections on Our Changing World*. University Park, PA: The Pennsylvania State University Press.

Castells, M. 1993. The Informational Economy and the New International Division of Labor. In *The New Global Economy in the Information Age: Reflections on Our Changing World* pp. 15–43. University Park, PA: The Pennsylvania State University Press.

Chick, V. 1983. *Macroeconomics After Keynes*. MIT Press.

Churchman, C. W. 1970. When Does a Model Represent Reality? In *The Process of Model Building in the Behavioral Sciences* pp. 133–138. Ohio State University Press.

Cleveland, H. 1982. Information as a Resource. *Futurist* 16(2):24–39.

Cooper, M. 1983. The Structure and Future of the Information Economy. *Information Processing and Management* 19(1):9–26.

Engler, N. January 25, 1999. Emerging Enterprise: Supply-Chain Help. *Information-Week*. Issue 718. 109.

Garson, G. D. 1995. *Computer Technology and Social Issues*. Harrisburg, PA: Idea Group Publishing.

Garcia, L. 1995. The Globalization of Telecommunications and Information. In W. J. Drake, (Ed.). *The New Information Infrastructure: Strategies for United States Policy* pp. 75–92. New York, NY: The Twentieth Century Fund Press.

Green, J. R. and Laffont, J. 1986. Incentive Theory with Data Compression. In W. Heller, R. M. and Starrett, D., (Eds.). *Uncertainty, Information and Communication, (Essays in honor of Kenneth J. Arrow, Volume III)* pp. 239–249. Cambridge University Press.

Goodman, S. 1987. The Information Technologies and Soviet Society: Problems and Prospects. *IEEE Transactions on Systems, Man and Cybernetics*. SMC-17(4), July–August:529–551.

Hayes, R. M. 1979. The Management of Library Resources: The Balance Between Capital and Staff in Providing Services. *Library Research* 1:119–142.

Haywood, T. 1995. *Info-Rich—Info-Poor. Access and Exchange in the Global Information Society*. London, UK: Bowker Saur.

Heller, W., Starr, R. M. and Starrett, D., (Eds.). 1986. *Uncertainty, Information and Communication, (Essays in honor of Kenneth J. Arrow, Volume III)*. Cambridge University Press.

Henderson, A. 1999. Information Science and Information Policy: The Use of Constant Dollars and Other Indicators to Manage Research Investments. *Journal of the American Society for Information Science* 50(4):366–379.

King, D. W., Roderer, N. K. and Olsen, H. A., (Eds.). 1983. *Key Papers in the Economics of Information*. White Plains, NY: American Society for Information Science, Knowledge Industry Publications, Inc.,

Kingma, B. R. 1996. *The Economics of Information: A Guide to Cost-Benefit Analysis for Information Professionals*. Englewood, CO: Libraries Unlimited.

Lamberton, D. M. 1983. National Policy for Economic Information. In D. W. King, N. K. Roderer and H. A. Olsen, (Eds.). *Key Papers in the Economics of Information* pp. 302–318. White Plains, NY: American Society for Information Science, Knowledge Industry Publications, Inc.

Lamberton, D. 1984. Economics of Information and Organization. *Annual Review of Information Science and Technology* 19:5–29.

Lancaster, F. W. 1971. The Cost-Effectiveness Analysis of Information Retrieval and Dissemination Systems. *Journal of the American Society for Information Science* pp. 12–27.

Lanvin, B. 1995. Why the Global Village Cannot Afford Information Slums. In W. J. Drake, (Ed.) *The New Information Infrastructure: Strategies for U. S. Policy* pp. 205–222. New York, NY: A Twentieth Century Fund Book.

Luce, R. D. 1970. What Are Mathematical Models of Behavior Models of ? In Stogdill, R.M., (Ed.), *The Process of Model Building in the Behavioral Sciences* pp. 115–132. Ohio State Press.

McCall, John J., (Ed.). 1982. *The Economics of Information and Uncertainty* (A Conference Report), University of Chicago Press.

Monthly Labor Review. April 1999. Computer Ownership up Sharply in the 1990's. Bureau of Labor Statistics. United States Department of Labor [online] http://stats.bls.gov/opub/ted/1999/apr/wk1/art01.htm

Morris, W. T. 1970. On the Art of Modeling. In *The Process of Model Building in the Behavioral Sciences* pp. 76–93. Ohio State University Press.

Myerson, R. B. 1986. Negotiations in Games: A Theoretical Overview. In W. Heller, M. R. Starr and D. Starrett, (Eds). *Uncertainty, Information and Communication, (Essays in honor of Kenneth J. Arrow, Volume III)* pp. 3–24. Cambridge University Press.

National Agricultural Statistics Services. USDA. 1999. Year 2000 Computerized Systems Readiness Report. [online] http://usda.mannlib.cornell.edu/usda/reports/nassr/other/computer/y2k0299.txt

Newman, G. 1983. An Institutional Perspective on Information. In D. W. King, N. K. Roderer and H. A. Olsen, (Eds.). *Key Papers in the Economics of Information* pp. 275–301. White Plains, NY: American Society for Information Science, Knowledge Industry Publications, Inc.

Nicolaidis, K. 1995. International Trade in Information-Based Services: The Uruguay Round and Beyond. In W. J. Drake, (Ed.) *The New Information Infrastructure: Strategies for United States Policy* pp. 269–303. New York, NY: The Twentieth Century Fund Press.

Nora, S. and Minc, A. 1980. *The Computerization of Society* pp vi–12. MIT Press.

Phlips, L. 1988. *The Economics of Imperfect Information*. Cambridge University Press.

Porter, M. E. and Millar, V. E. 1985. How Information Gives You Competitive Advantage. *Harvard Business Review* July–August:149–160.

Redman, B. J. and Redman, J. C. 1981. *Microeconomic: Resource Allocation and Price Theory*. Westport, CT: AVI Publishing.

Robinson, S. 1986. Analyzing the Information Economy: Tools and Techniques. *Information Processing and Management* 22(3):183–202.

Rothschild, M. 1986. Asset Pricing Theories. In W. Heller, M. R. Starr and D. Starrett, (Eds.) *Uncertainty, Information and Communication, (Essays in honor of Kenneth J. Arrow, Volume III)*. pp. 97–128. Cambridge University Press.

Rubin, M. R. and Sapp, M. E. 1981. Selected Roles of Information Goods and Services in the United States National Economy. *Information Processing and Management* 17, 1981: 195–213.

Schiller, D. 1988. How to Think about Information. In Moscoe and Wasco, (Eds.) *The Political Economy of Information* pp. 27–42. University of Wisconsin Press.

Shannon, C. E. and Weaver, W. 1949. *The Mathematical Theory of Communication*. Urbana, IL: University of Illinois Press.

Smith, J. M. 1982. *Evolution and the Theory of Games*. New York, NY: Cambridge University Press.

Spink, A. 1997. Study of Interactive Feedback during Mediated Information Retrieval. *Journal of the American Society for Information Science* 48(5):382–394.

Starr, M. R. and Starrett, D., (Eds.). 1986. *Uncertainty, Information and Communication, (Essays in honor of Kenneth J. Arrow, Volume III)*. pp. 239–253. Cambridge University Press.

Stein, T. and Sweat, J. November 9, 1998. Killer Supply Chains. [online] http://www/informationweek.com/708/08iukil.htm

Stogdill, R. M. 1970. Introduction: The Student and Model Building. In *The Process of Model Building in the Behavioral Sciences*. Ohio State University Press.

Tapscott, D. 1996. *The Digital Economy: Promise and Peril in the Age of Networked Intelligence*. New York, NY: McGraw-Hill.

Villano, M. March, 15, 1999. A Lead-Pipe Cinch. *CIO* 12(11):51–60.

Wilkin, A. 1977. Personal Roles and Barriers in Information Transfer. *Advances in Librarianship* 7:257–297.

# Chapter 7

# Interpretations of Value

## Introduction

Establishing the value of information has presented complex and unique problems for economists and information scientists for most of this century (King, Roderer and Olsen, 1983). Defining information and relating it to a value, a benefit, or cost structure have so far presented significant theoretical problems. Information value, if characterized as being measured as the usefulness or utility of information, cannot usually be ascribed until after the information has been obtained and applied. This presents a paradox: how to place a value on information and how to measure that value cannot necessarily be accomplished at the same stage of economic interplay. In fact, when information is valued in this fashion, dependent upon the usefulness of information, the value can be as dependent on the recipient of the information as the information itself (King et al.; Repo, 1983).

Various attempts have been made over the years to confront these fundamental issues. In 1945, Hayek discussed the market mechanism as a way in which information is valued. In 1966, Boulding presented ideas of how information is individually valued. Marschack (1968) attempted to use a Shannon-like model to define information in economic terms. Kenneth Arrow (1984) recognized information as an entity, integrally linked to uncertainty and economics, in need of clearer definition and valuation. Fritz Machlup (1979) examined the issues involved in measuring the value of information and offered several cost-benefit analysis considerations for use in this effort. Historically, these authors have created the paths used to review information value and attempted to cope with the complexities of the value of information.

Attempts to clarify the definition of information to attend to the issue of valuing it have engaged economists and information scientists in cost-benefit analysis discussions, commodity versus resource debates, probability theory, game theory, and multitudes of various other controversies (King et al., 1983; Repo, 1983; Bates, 1988; Arrow, 1984; Cleveland, 1982; Spence, 1974). Debates over the appropriateness of neoclassical economic considerations in describing the value of information and adventures into Keynesian and Baysian models have only served to further complicate the discussion (Newman, 1983; Lamberton, 1983). Essentially, all of these inquiries have contributed to describing information and information value, which might eventually yield a working, though probably not a definitive approach to the issues involved. Re-examining some aspects and suggesting some alternative interpretations may provide a path to additional insight into the issues of information value. Key to any discussion of information value has to be the context of the consideration, which is one of the areas that economic modeling tends to simplify beyond recognition. Actual information value is steeped in enormous context, built by the actors, the environment, and the anticipated, or hoped for, outcomes. Without an understanding of these aspects it is too easy to inappropriately interpret an economic exchange.

## Value in Context

Value refers to the worth, utility, or desirability, which is assumed, demonstrated, or bestowed upon an entity, activity, or product (utility equals use or usefulness). Whether the thing being valued is a commodity or a resource has no specific tangible effect on the value. The overall status as a scarce resource, or an essential commodity, or a socially prized item may affect the trading price or exchange value, but the conditions of quantity and social opinion are the precipitous factors, not whether it is a thing of nature or a product of man. (Repo, 1983; Bickner, 1983). *The value of information, regardless of whether it is considered a commodity or a resource, is the worth, utility, or desirability that is assumed about it, demonstrated by it, or bestowed upon it.* How is the value ascertained and how is it measured? How is the worth of information determined in selling, purchasing, or otherwise obtaining that information? How is that worth, that value, measured and acted upon? Information value is relative. It is dependent upon the *identity, role, or orientation* of the potential users and the information relationship to, or within, a specific identity at a specific time. Identity characteristics may include cultural, personal, and organizational components. The term cultural is used to refer to ethnic background and involvement. Personal refers to individual; that is, though influenced by cultural considerations, not being wholly based upon the group, though personal and cultural components may be inextricably connected. Organizational means whatever structured environment the individual or culture may function within. Fundamental to a discussion of value of information in this context is the assertion that the value of information is tied to the individuals, cultures, or organizations and thereby to an identity, role, or orientation related to those aspects.

Traditions, information about the conduct of a particular group, pass from one generation to another as the continuance of a body of information that separates one culture from another. This conveyance may involve an individual as the medium, as in the carrying of oral histories over the generations. The value of information, in this case being culturally based, is prized as central to the congruity of the group's past, present, and future; the information is essentially priceless to the cultural entity and to the individuals that comprise that body. As such, the information is reproduced generation to generation, as children reproduce the genetic traits of parents, reproduced information carries the traditions and histories of cultures. And just like the occasional aberration of an inherited trait, information can be affected by the reproduction. Information might have NO value outside the cultural boundaries. Cultures may prize information that has no utility outside that culture, or has no correspondent outside the culture, or simply has no meaning taken out of the context of the specific culture. In this case, the information value *appears* sterile; it has no external value and no external reproduction is likely.

The error in this is that even information that is not valued across cultures may be personally valued. A visitor to a culture hears a traditional story and carries it to other situations, to other cultures. Personal valuation of information will be based on personal interests, characteristics, education, history, etc. Personal views affect the value placed on information in a personal role and influence areas of agreement with the information. Concepts of self-image and group association will play a significant part in how the information is personally valued (Boulding, 1973) and reproduced.

## Renovation and Mutation of Information

Information transmitted out of its original corpus may be modified by the new carrier, either by intention, (*renovation of information*) or by accident (*mutation of information*). In renovation of information, intentional modification is undertaken, such as adjusting all books to use politically correct gender descriptors; this changes the information conveyed and depending on which side of the issue one stands, changes the value placed upon that information. Individuals may inject personal value into information value. Value can be changed when information is added, subtracted, or interpreted. When information is interpreted or applied interpretatively, it is modified and may increase or decrease in value. Attempting to change culturally valued information will be met with resistance, and such modified information will be devalued. External to the cultural base, interpretation may provide value, real or imagined, to information that is otherwise sterile outside of the cultural frame. One culture's interpretation of another culture's traditions may add value to the information about another culture, regardless of the correctness of the interpretation. Interest in the artifacts of another culture denotes information value associated with what can be determined about that other culture, but modern interpretations, no matter how well grounded in sustained research, may still be incorrect. However, until the information is disputed, the information value, assigned in this instance by an external culture, will be based upon criteria of the external culture. The external culture's interpretation may be considered sterile, relative to information value by the original culture.

Mutation of information occurs when information received is unintentionally modified through carrier failure, such as a bad phone connection. Mutation may be the result of misinterpretation of information as well. Renovation and mutation of information produce changes that may influence the value of information. Either occurrence could yield new information with new value. An error in a chemical formula could yield a new compound with higher information value than the original formula. An error in interpretation might lead to a different set of ideas and discoveries and have a different resulting information value, which could be positive or negative.

## Organization and Value

Organizational components to be considered in valuing information are related to the structures that may affect the movement of information and the interpretations that the organizational body may attempt to force on information. Information value in the organization is determined by specific characteristics of the organization. Team organization versus top-down organization will influence how information is valued and how it is transmitted or not transmitted. Management formations, or cultural hierarchies, contribute to information value. Top-down styles keep the lower echelons less informed; there is less information available. If neo-classical supply and demand models are applied to information, this would increase information value in general, but information is not well suited to those models and frequently the information drifting down in top-down management systems is considered less valuable than other sources. Team management or cooperative management systems may have varying information value ranges based on the actual degree of trust among the cooperative units, and the ability to transmit information intact, as these systems have more channels for transmission and verification than top-down. The sources of information that an organization group finds acceptable will influence information value. If the information sources are all external or all internal, or any extremely imbalanced configuration thereof, the information may be drastically skewed and the value of the information should then be appraised with extreme caution. However, if organizational information gathering techniques are skewed, it may not be possible for that organization to recognize that information value will be skewed as well.

The organizational component of identity is not limited to businesses or single cultures. The organization of a multicultural society, such as our own, influences how information is valued, in that information movement is affected by the structures of our society, and interpretations are imposed upon information by our information media. In certain groups, the information value of the front page of *The New York Times* is considered significantly greater than the information value of *USA Today*; in other groups the opposite valuation is made. In parts of the academic world, the organizational structure rewards seekers of new information with little regard to the value of that information. In fact, in the research realm the organization creates a special information value problem. Researchers may seek to maintain exclusive knowledge of information, prizing the information based on possible future value that is accrued by having exclusive credit for the discovery of the information. The information has value as a credential for the researcher, possibly even significant financial benefit. However, the information value may be even higher in the general knowledge base, as was the case for a number of discoveries regarding acquired immune deficiency syndrome (AIDS) and how it is transmitted. There are risks involved with information value, both in the application and in the attempt. Such risks include placing value on what is valuable only to a closed culture, or undervaluing information because it is misunderstood but is later clarified and found to be of extreme value. What must be recognized is that any information valuation system is composed of more than just information issues. There is a significant amount of scenario relativity; that is, who, what, where, and why should influence how any measures for information value are applied.

## Measurability

Some aspects of information are measurable, i.e., values can be derived from the construction of a database based on cost-benefit analysis. How many person-hours, how much computer equipment, how much electricity, how much paper, essentially, how much production and labor capital was put into the construction of the database can be determined. But what is the value of the information in the database, not the database entity, but the information it contains? Repo contends that "criteria for the determination of the value of information arise out of the process of use and seeking of it" ( 1983, p. 376). He further proposes that there are criteria for utilization—validity, quality, ease of use, and the degree of fit between the information provided and the environment in which it is being sought. This utility value is certainly valid after the database has been purchased, but how does the purchaser determine the value of information before it is purchased? The value of the information in the purchaser's eyes is important prior to purchase because it is contributory to the decision to purchase, as well as contributing to factors that will influence price acceptance. Basically, the purchaser needs information about the information in the database to make the decision to purchase. (This aspect of information is reduction of uncertainty at purchase. The database, it is assumed, is desired to assist in reduction of other uncertainty.) This need for information about the information is where the problem of the value of information is most complex, though it may appear simple. In the case of databases, it is possible to use pre-established criteria in evaluating the potential usefulness of a database. But, the criteria may be based upon a level playing field; that is, that the representative database samples reflect the actual database content. If a database is actually electronic yellow pages, is that the database content anticipated when purchasing a targeted mailing list?

When purchasing a house, the buyer has made certain assumptions about the quality of the materials used in the structure, the quality of the workmanship, the longevity of the electrical systems, furnace and so on. Those assumptions are made, however, under certain contractual agreements that guarantee performance for a specified period of time. The buyer is accepting the risk that the builder can be held to the terms of the contract if something goes wrong with the house or with the finances of the contractor. Through legal agreement and the acceptance of some risk, the buyer is relying on the contractor and the courts to protect his or her investment in the house. The buyer purchases the house after inspection of it, but unless he or she was able to monitor every step of the construction process, inspect the products used, and knew enough about the whole method of construction, it is still a risk; the purchase is made based on uncertainty, to an extent the buyer is accepting a lack of information. Is this different from the purchase of the database, or of information in general? The buyer does not really know the performance level of the house until it's used. The purchaser does not really know the performance level of the information until it is used.

Further, if the purchaser fails to use the information or fails to apply the information most profitably, is it the vendor's fault? What if the purchaser uses the information to create yet another product that yields significant financial benefit to the original purchaser but no benefit to the original seller? These are issues of copyright and intellectual property. However, consider again the house: the contractor built and sold it. Now the buyer owns it. What if he or she adds a room, a pool, or redecorates? Can the builder claim a right to the increased value made of the house? No, the builder cannot.

## Averaging Anticipated Value

Purchasers of information must make more complex decisions about information than about physical materials. Anticipated value or anticipated benefit of information must be considered. Determining an appropriate value may be attempted by calculating "...an average of all the possible values of some good or outcome weighted by their respective likelihood" (Bates, 1988, p. 78). Estimating all the possible values from the use of information and adjusting for the likelihood that such use will occur allows for consideration for variations in value based upon context of use and the possibility of other uses of the information. This method, in theory, would provide a way to allow "the analyst to treat the value of information goods as fixed in subsequent analyses" (p. 78), having the advantage of such a value based upon the probability of applications permits a balance of exchange values to be considered. These types of considerations are taken into account when purchasing a house or a computer or any other marketable entity. To some extent, using this type of valuation technique with information requires more comprehensive understanding of what the information has to accomplish and what possible outcomes may be obtained.

## Lack of Prior Knowledge

What if the information that the purchaser needs is something he does not have any prior experience with, or any prior data or estimations about? The "black box" of high school science class comes to mind: how does the purchaser know how to value what is in the black box without knowing anything about the contents? This is the recurring question, how does a purchaser, or vendor, determine value of a black box, an unknown? This is the issue that has not yet been adequately answered. Despite the similarities between purchasing a house and purchasing information, there is the overriding, recurring issue of the depth of unknown referent to information. Information can be as simple as a house, a database from a reputable vendor who has identified precisely the depth of the data in the database, or information can be a black box. A black box is the unknown that is exposed when experimenting in science laboratories. How does one place value on the information created, acquired or stumbled across in a laboratory experiment?

Many new products and much new information emerged from the NASA programs to reach the moon. Many of the products were the result of attempting to solve specific problems identified in the preparation for the flights. Commodities and information were created to address specific problems. Some of the solutions discovered addressed tangential issues or had larger economic advantages, such as Velcro. The many computer applications of hardware and software and medical data also yielded side benefits, which we reap to this day. The value of the information to be gained in the effort was not known. There was an assumption of risk, an acceptance of uncertainty in venturing into the experiment. The people involved in the experiment, the agencies providing funding, and to some extent the general populace of the United States assumed that the information would be valuable—that is, it would be useful. It is often with this perception, or prediction of value, that value is implied. Value so derived may be overestimated or underestimated. In an economic view, determining the value of information remains a high-risk proposition that requires more information to reduce uncertainty.

## Cost Benefit Analysis

The interrelatedness of information value within a potential context or application suggests the appropriate approach to valuing information should be constructed around cost-benefit analysis. A working analysis of this type would involve the creation of a scenario documenting the environment of the information application, including all the potential contributing costs coupled with estimations of potential benefit. The difficulty originates from identifying cost accurately and estimating benefits reasonably. To fully determine a value in this variety of systems, it is necessary to include the elusive "public good" notions typically associated with the communications arena.

Let us examine one example. The cost of placing computers into grade schools should include the cost of the machines, the modification to the electrical systems, long-term change in the cost of building utilities, costs for paper, wiring, maintenance, plus the cost of training teachers to be able to use the systems and to teach the students. The cost of training seems to be always overlooked, but more than that is the cost involved in bringing computers into the curriculum in a meaningful way with tangible results for the students and the teachers. There is no question that there is value involved in the provision of the machines and the related information, but the value cannot be calculated without taking into account all the actual costs, even the ones economists like to overlook because they make the equations ungainly. The issue of benefit or measurable value can only be accurately determined if all the potential results are estimated. If the teachers are trained to use the equipment to teach the students, the investment in the teachers is recovered in one teaching cycle and will not need repeating if successfully accomplished the first time. With the teachers trained, it can be assumed that they will continue to grow as they teach, so the value of the initial training will in the long run at least be worth twice the initial investment. The equipment will degrade over time, but if it is used to its fullest, integrated into the curriculum so that students and teachers are maximizing results, the depreciation would be appropriate over time and still be a benefit as even an old system is useful when properly integrated and managed. The alternative, that is, not having put the equipment into the classroom, or not having trained the teachers adequately would mean no benefit. Simply, training twenty teachers, who train twenty more students each for five years, means 2,000 students trained with the technology who would have more opportunity than 2,000 students with no such experience. In a cost-benefit analysis, this can be distilled to numbers, but the environment and larger outcome must be considered to fully anticipate a value. Estimating values in this fashion is cumbersome but may be useful in reducing uncertainty or at least anticipating potential utility. This framework permits the insertion of the cultural or organizational elements, which may so dramatically influence a value situation.

## Summary

Information value is intrinsically bound to the transmitter, the receiver, and the channel in specific relation to their identity models and their situations. The utility of any information, and therefore the value of information, is situationally bound. Understanding the possible components involved and preparing scenario analyses may enable the establishment of valuation parameters relative to specific characteristic components. Without comprehending the relativity of information value, we will not satisfactorily address the issue.

# References

Arrow, K. J. 1984. *Collected Papers of Kenneth J. Arrow: The Economics of Information, Volume 4*. Cambridge, MA: Belknap Press of Harvard University Press.

Bates, B. 1988. Information as an Economic Good: Sources of Individual and Social Value. In Mosco and Wasco. *The Political Economy of Information* pp. 76–94.

Bickner, R. E. 1983. Concepts of Economics. In D. W. King, N. K. Roderer and H. A. Olsen, (Eds.). *Key Papers in the Economics of Information* pp. 10-49. White Plains, NY: Knowledge Industry Publications.

Boulding, K. 1973. *The Image*. The University of Michigan Press.

King, D.W., Roderer, N.K., and Olsen, H.A., (Eds.) 1983. *Key Papers in the Economics of Information*. White Plains, NY: Knowledge Industry Publications.

Lamberton, D. M. 1983. National Policy for Economic Information. In D. W. King, N. K. Roderer and H. A. Olsen, (Eds) *Key Papers in the Economics of Information* pp. 302–318. White Plains, NY: Knowledge Industry Publications.

Machlup, F. September 1979. Uses, Value, and Benefits of Knowledge. *Knowledge*. vol. 1. (1):62–81. Sage.

Marschak, J. May 1968. Economics of Inquiring, Communication, Deciding. *American Economic Review*. vol. 58. In T. Saracevic, (Ed.) 1970. *Introduction to Information Science* pp. 697–706. New York, NY: R. R. Bowker.

Newman, G. 1983. Institutional Perspective on Information. In D. W. King, N. K. Roderer and H. A. Olsen, (Eds) *Key Papers in the Economics of Information* pp. 275–301. White Plains, NY: Knowledge Industry Publications.

Repo, A. 1983. The Dual Approach to the Value of Information: An Appraisal of Use and Exchange Values. *Information Processing and Management* 22(5):373–383.

Spence, A. M. 1974. An Economist's View of Information. *Annual Review of Information Science and Technology* vol. 9, pp. 57–78.

# Chapter 8

# Digital Accessibility: Information Value in Changing Hierarchies

*Co-author: June Lester*

## Introduction

With access to authority levels merely a few keystrokes away, the rigid managerial hierarchy has experienced contractions of layers. Increased and nearly instant access as well as heightened expectations for responses creates demands for attention, which may impact management itself. Planning to provide more resources in the digital age requires new forms of resource control techniques, including better time management and evaluation of information value. So many voices can now be heard that new structures and economies must be considered. Addressing all the needs of all the players on the digital information field will require some creativity. Will the modified management structures be able to address the digital revolution?

This chapter addresses the concept of information value in organizations and how that value is impacted and displayed by two different but related aspects of digital accessibility:

1. the impact of digital accessibility on the organizational hierarchy and the resulting effect on information value;

2. the possible differentiation in information value resulting both from variations in the pace of infusion of information technology into the organization and differing attitudes toward the positioning and extent of expenditures on information technology by the organization.

In the first aspect, the discussion will show how change in access leads to changes in the organizational structure for information gathering, resulting in

109

an increase in information used for decision making and greater value placed on information both from within and without the organization, and how change in access leads to differing valuations of information. In the second aspect, the discussion will focus on the interplay of the pace, extent, and structure of information technology infusion within the organizational hierarchy and the resulting impact on access to information channels and valuing of information. The purpose here is to raise issues for consideration, not to provide answers.

## Impact of Digital Accessibility on the Organizational Hierarchy

Organizational structure is an information transfer system designed to service groups or individuals to permit the completion of the tasks and missions of the organization (Nadler, 1992). As Kaltnekar states, "Organizational relations are defined by information and vice versa. In fact, organization processes mainly represent various activities relative to information: input, processing, transmission and above all numerous information flows connected with it" (1991, p. 516). Typically, until the advent of modern information technology, this was a relatively inflexible hierarchical channel through which information flowed, or sometimes trickled, dependent upon one's position in the channel. The role of the individual or group within the organization fairly well dictated the level, quality, and character of the information access available. The position of an individual in a specific location in the channel also tended to form the image, or self-perception, which the individual held of his or her role in the organization and even lent to the creation of an image of the organization itself (Gardner and Peluchette, 1991). The combined images of self and organizational structures worked together to form the basis for the interactions of the individual with the organization. The individual needed to know whom to directly approach for information, and who had to be approached via a series of other individuals. That is, what channels of authority had to be followed in communications. Further, these combined images influenced the methods used in hierarchical communications. Speaking with one's immediate supervisor might be acceptable for addressing some issues; other issues required written communications. In either case, the individual's style of presentation and interaction was affected by the perceptions of both self-role and the organizational structure (Gardner and Peluchette).

Concomitant to these perceptions of role and structure is the notion of organizational culture, which includes the history and environment that formed the existing communications pathways (Nadler and Tushman, 1992). The value ascribed to any communications up or down the channel can be impacted by any or all of these components. For example, an individual's position in the hierarchy attaches certain value to information regardless of the actual value. The structure, the layers of authority, the hierarchy of communication, the style and method of presentation, the players and their roles—all these contribute to the information system of an organization, and each component influences the valuing of the information communicated through that system.

The information or communications system is the infrastructure base of the organization, is a major reason for having a formal structure (Gerstein, 1992), and is key to the decision-making functions of the organization (Kaltnekar, 1991). This system has been profoundly affected by the advent of information technology. According to Nadler, "Information technology has begun to revolutionize organizational design by providing alternatives to hierarchy as the primary means of coordination" (1992, p. 5) and information transfer. Nadler also talks about several variations on the traditional organization that have emerged:

1. self-managed teams

2. high performance work systems that emphasize the integration of advanced tools like expert systems with modified worker organizations

3. increased joint ventures between companies

4. greater collaboration inside and outside organizations

5. outsourcing

Essentially, the evolution of computer technology, and especially networking systems, has impacted every aspect of the traditional organization. Electronic mail, electronic bulletin boards, shared files, and other similar systems allow information transfer without the typical channels of hierarchy, breaking down rigid organizational structures by circumventing that hierarchy and allowing information to flow through the electronic structure rather than through the traditional one. This openness is what allows organizations to expand the personnel involved in projects and to network outside of themselves. Boundaries become blurred, both within the work groups and within the organization. Decision making becomes less centralized, more dispersed, and certainly at some levels, less institutional in nature (Kaltnekar, 1991). The composition of the organization changes. Over time even the "walls" of the organization change to encompass the customers within the evolving information net. As some organizations have experienced, the voice, or rather e-mail, of the customers can indeed cause them to appear to be interior to the organization. Fifty percent of respondents to a *Computerworld* magazine survey reported they measure "the performance of information technology by asking their . . . customers for feedback" and "92 percent of them have data communications links with their customers" (Rayner, 1995, p. 8).

The potential for such close contact, whether among customers and organizations or workers within organizations, can have both positive and negative consequences. It may be assumed that despite the ability to do so, individuals will not rashly travel outside the bounds of the traditional structures and will not skip all the levels of the hierarchy to satisfy a desire to communicate directly with the ultimate boss, but there is actually little beyond common sense and organizational culture to prevent this. Though face to face encounters between the extremes of the hierarchy would be unlikely, or confined to very specific situational circumstances, electronic encounters are not so constrained. Customer contact into organizations was expanded substantially just by the general introduction of the telephone.

The newest technology, along with changing views of the criticality of the customer, seems to be opening more communication avenues to all levels of the organization. Customers can have near instant access to an organization via the Web or e-mail, and what they cannot access they certainly can and do discuss. Failure to respond can be devastating: as an example, one computer producer able to handle only 4,000 of the 10,000 calls a day being received was attacked on the Internet, with messages of complaint and displeasure that cost the company "more than half of the company's sales-related input and...lost business" (DeYoung, 1995, p. 42). More recently, surveys by *InformationWeek* indicate nearly 75 percent of the senior executives are making customer service and management a higher priority (Thyfault, Johnston and Sweat, October 1998, online).

In recent years there has been significant growth in the use of the Internet, particularly the graphical Web, in order to share and gather information with potential customers. The advent of improved browsers and relatively easy HTML authoring tools has enhanced the ability of organizations to create sites and has increased the pressure to have a presence on the Web. Increasingly organizations use the Web as a distribution site for their products, information, or surveying activities. Estimating that more than 80 million consumers in the United States alone access the Web for information about emerging products, potential purchases, reviews, and service reports means opportunities for closer contact for the customers and the manufacturers. Monitoring the activities of the customer on the Web sites can provide early signs of purchasing habits or changes in customer attitudes. General Motors has been able to use these sites to make more information about their vehicles, purchasing and leasing plans available to customers. These types of sites help to build customer loyalty and help the manufacturer to review plans and evaluate how customers react to changes (Szygenda, 1999, online).

Universities are creating Web sites to recruit prospective students, to provide online admission applications, and to provide information about courses, schedules, degree programs, and conference meetings. Nonprofit organizations use Web sites to provide online contact points for volunteers. Individuals advertise their services and products. Federal and state government agencies and cities as well are putting up an electronic presence, providing access for their constituents. Incorporation of this information technology into the information transfer system is rapidly becoming ubiquitous as part of the organizational structure across all sectors, with significant impact on information flow and information value.

Today we are in an environment in which consumers are responsive and insistent and expect feedback as quickly as they can type in requests. Repeat e-mail messages come less than ten minutes apart, as senders expect a resolution of their issues immediately. Messages or postings appear that seem to assume everyone else in the world is attending to e-mail or bulletin boards at the same time. Organizations and individual employees are having to devise schemes to provide timely responses to even the most trivial electronic inquiry, because any message can be the predicator of a public display of anger, a public haranguing that can cost consumer confidence, or a frenzy of complaints from others who have felt slighted but who were not previously motivated to report. Electronic accessibility is inserting the consumer, the customer, or even just the casual, unrelated computer user into the structure of any organization that has assumed an electronic presence.

The impact of this electronic information stream varies. Out of self-defense some administrators, high profile scientists, CEOs, and the like make public announcements that they do not respond directly to e-mail. One obvious problem with the electronic system is the time one must invest to keep current with the messages, to keep one's message spaces uncluttered. Neither time nor space necessarily impacts electronic communications, so long as the system is accessible.

Several questions arise in reference to this changing scene, in which there is increased accessibility both from within the organization and from the outside to the decision-making levels of the organization:

1. How does one manage the impact of this changed information system on the organization?

2. What channels of communication need to be kept in place, and which are obsolete, if indeed any are?

3. What information value system will be in place, and how will it differ from the information value system of the hierarchical organization?

4. If customers are to be internally involved in the organization, what are the boundaries, if there are any?

Most organizations have changed, but despite the predictions since the 1960s, that information technology would decrease the levels of hierarchy and flatten the structure significantly, flattened is probably not the appropriate interpretation of what has occurred. Though organizations have decreased the layers of hierarchy by one or two levels (Shimada, 1991), this has not positioned everyone on the same stairs of the hierarchy. Decision making may be more distributed due to improved technology but it is not horizontal.

Methods of communication and channels for control of communication have changed not only in relation to the increased technology, but also in relation to changes in the larger social environment. Information technology allows anyone with access to communicate with anyone else in the network. However, the organizational culture and common sense can serve to control these communications relatively well. Agreed upon standards and procedures for the use of electronic mail as well as other communication systems channels can limit inappropriate use. Just as there are rules to govern the use of phones in the workplace, or appropriate procedures for filing a complaint, similar rules and procedures can be delineated related to the use of information technology.

Although enhanced digital accessibility may have the potential of providing total elimination of hierarchical information flow, removal of all the channels for control of communication could cause chaos. Whatever minimal control channels are necessary to provide organizational structure need to be maintained, but with enough flexibility to allow communications advantageous to the organization. The issue of valuing the information that is to be communicated through the electronic systems has to be confronted at various levels. From without, customer input can help identify new markets or point out repairable shortcomings. From within, members of the organization may see things that others miss, which could lead to new opportunities. As always, determining what information is valuable is dependent on factors far beyond the control of the sender and often not fully understood by the recipient. So long as no information is discarded without examination, there is at least some chance that items of value will not be lost. The task of examining all incoming information can overwhelm, undermining the ability to recognize valuable information.

The increase in customer information that results from the juncture of digital accessibility, increased responsiveness to customer needs, and enhanced customer orientation as the focus of the organization poses significant challenges in managing information flow and in assessing information value. Streamlining information is more easily achieved in managing employee input, limiting communication and reports to what is determined to be critical, but it is not possible to completely streamline customer input. The use of online surveys helps to delineate some of the customer input, but none of it can be overlooked. As mentioned before, ignoring customer input can be a costly error.

The issue of boundaries for customers involved internally in the organization is in some ways a very difficult issue. Whether it is a for-profit or nonprofit organization, the consumer public can sow havoc when dissatisfied. Between the phone and the computer, there are few limits to the contacts the public can make, and using a global medium like the Internet can certainly lend volume to one's words. Being able to e-mail the CEO or the President grants a sense of democratic power, but such power is not always responsibly exercised. How to cope with what might be serious charges or just angry misinterpretations is a challenge.

Each organization will make decisions about these challenges predicated on the customer base, the receptivity to customer input, the ability to divine the real from the unreal. The bottom line is that the customer cannot be ignored, must never be insulted, and should always be listened to. What happens after that is completely situationally dependent. The wise organization will have some means to analyze and evaluate the various situations arising from customer intervention in information flow. The boundaries will have to be set by the organization, but without a doubt those boundaries will be challenged.

## Variations in the Pace of Infusion of Information Technology into the Organization

In addition to the increased accessibility provided by electronic systems and the resulting change in information flow and value within an organization, another significant factor influencing changes in information flow has been the practice of not providing every member of the organization with access to the information technology necessary to participate in the new communication systems, often with cost as a justification for this selective dissemination approach. Despite the tremendous growth in availability of information technology, there is still a discrepancy between the media hype and the actual installation of information technology in organizations.

These transitional organizational states, where information technology is not fully installed or implemented, can have negative effects on the organization at both macro and micro levels. At the macro level, because there has been global growth in the implementation of information technology as a resource expanding tool, organizations ignoring information technology or not fully utilizing it risk losing markets, limiting growth potential, and failing to recognize and exploit opportunities. On the micro level, individuals without information technology access are limited in job growth, job security, future employment potential, and critical information. Diminished workers who are not keeping current ultimately cost organizations in a variety of arenas. Individuals without information resources cannot contribute to the organization at the same level as other workers. Workers without the technology are relegated to the traditional hierarchy, whereas those with technology access have access to the changing style of decision making. In the marketplace, consumers with technology access can impact organizations, but since the actual demographics of the computer-owning public are still not known, the impact is difficult to control or predict. The whole arena is still evolving and new enough that it is not reasonable to characterize the computer-user population, especially as online services make access easier for less technologically oriented people.

Within the organization, information technology access is not just the possession of the machines; it also involves having or acquiring appropriate technical skills. Training and currency with information technology is considered critical by workers for job satisfaction and likewise critical by employers seeking to maintain a stable, functional information systems workforce (Earls, 1995). Within organizations, an artificial hierarchy based on possession of and skill with technology is created, and such an artificial structure impedes an organization's (or a society's) growth through negative impacts related to the differential valuing of information technology in comparison with other factors. Undeserved stature may be accorded to information that is transferred using the new technology, while information that is transmitted by traditional means or through the traditional hierarchy may be falsely devalued. The possession of technical skills may give individuals additional rank and authority, while diminishing the rank and authority of less technically skilled workers, regardless of other career-related criteria. Sometimes the trade-off is the loss of years of organizational knowledge and culture, as in the early retirement of key workers who for a variety of reasons are not given access to the technology or are not provided with training. While such retirements are often viewed positively, the changing organization structure may not be as well positioned as some may think. The information lost with those types of retirements cannot be replaced or recouped by technology. The insight that a longtime employee might have into the current and future activities of an organization based upon the time in place and experiential knowledge is lost, and the value of this lost information may be unrecognized potential diversification or missed market opportunities.

Information technology staff are not necessarily in possession of enough information to appropriately outfit the entire organization, and the devaluing of nontechnologically generated information may have long-term consequences. The unreasonable expectation that the information technology staff should be able to understand every individual task of the organization may have led to the unmet expectations of the early information technology years. More realistically, successful organizations are encouraging the involvement of non-information technology staff in information technology acquisitions, design, and implementation. This two-fold strategy empowers the employee while investing him or her in the job and recognizes a diversity of information values. Determining, with help from the information technology staff, what hardware and software will best help perform the job, causes the employee to take responsibility and also commits her or him to the organization (Kaltnekar, 1991).

## Differing Approaches to Expenditures on Information Technology

Revamping, upgrading, or expanding organizations are spending large sums of money on information technology initiatives. In 1994, the per employee expenditures by the top 100 outstanding users of client/server information technology worldwide, located primarily in the developed world, ranged from $27,442 in the financial services sector, to $19,815 in the insurance industry, and $10,170 in telecommunications (Rayner, 1995).

One might suppose that this pattern of expenditure on information technology would engender enormous information systems staff, creating yet another layer of management and a modern subhierarchy. Two different surveys conducted by *Computerworld* provide information about information technology users. One survey identified 100 outstanding information technology users, representing a global listing of organizations, and the other survey produced a list of the 100 best United States-based managers of information. From the Computerworld 100 Global Users surveys it is possible to examine the potential for significant information system subhierarchies as indicated by the amounts of money and the number of employees dedicated to information technology. ABB (Asea Brown Boveri Limited), a Swiss industrial equipment company with $28 billion in revenues, has 5,000 information system employees and spends $700 million on information system services. Charles Schwab Corporation, with a revenue of $1.06 billion, spends between $100 and $250 million on information systems services and employs between 500 and 1,000 information system workers. CSX, the railroad transportation, maintenance and repair organization, employs 1,200 information systems personnel and spends $160 million on information systems out of a $9.5 billion revenue. Eli Lilly, the American pharmaceutical giant with revenues of $6.45 billion, employs 2,500–5,000 information systems workers and spends between $250 and $500 million on information systems and services. Ford Motor Company likewise employs 2,500–5,000 information systems workers while spending between $250–500 million, but on revenues of $108 billion (Malloy, 1995). Although the surveys do not provide much insight into the composition or distribution of these employees, with such numbers it is impossible to believe that there are not information systems divisions and departments within these organizations.

Other organizations appear to be moving in a different direction. Outback Steak House, which moved into information technology in 1992 with a system it contends provides only information that is meaningful to the restaurant managers, employs an information system staff of less than 100 people to assist a business with revenues of $451 million. Western National Corp, "a leader in the annuity business, managing assets in excess of $8.6 billion" has an information systems staff of eleven people (McWilliams, 1995, p. 24). Neither Outback Steak House nor Western National has an executive in charge of information systems. A vice president of Western National expresses their philosophy this way: "We don't want to bottleneck [information management] through one person or one department, such that if you want information you have to go to them" (p. 24). Of Western National Corp. revenues of $615 million, less than 1 percent, $4.9 million, is spent on information systems (Computerworld Premier 100, 1995, p. 46). Notably, the majority of organizations on the Premier 100 list, the Computerworld survey of U.S. companies with the highest information productivity, are primarily smaller businesses with revenues under $1 billion (McWilliams, 1995, pp. 7, 46-53). The average information system expenditure of this Premier 100 list was 2.6 percent of revenue, with 34 companies below 1 percent (p. 40). Remarks from the information technology heads of some of the Global 100 list, the outstanding users of information technology list, indicate an understanding of the cooperative role they play in an organization. The division head of systems and technology for BankExim, a limited liability commercial bank located in Indonesia, reports that "to make the best use of each department's strengths, she encourages flexibility and joint projects. A rigid structure would isolate the departments and undermine the goal of the organization" (Malloy, 1995, p. 57). Other information technology managers' remarks include keeping sight of the company's objectives and recognizing that sometimes the option not to further automate is valid (Malloy).

Sweat and Hibbard (June 21, 1999) report that while expenditures on customer service and related software expanded from $200 million to over $1 billion between 1994 and 1997, indicators of customer satisfaction derived from the Customer Satisfaction Index fell from 74.5 to 70.1 during the same time period. Research conducted by *InformationWeek* revealed that the 300 information technology executives surveyed ranked 'understanding and meeting customer needs' and 'improved customer service' "as the top two technology and business priorities" (p. 68). This is not surprising since there appears to be a correlation between the scores received on the customer satisfaction index and stock values (p. 68).

The differential patterns of expenditure suggest possible differential valuing of information among the organizations. Should such a conclusion rest on the premise that the valuing of information by the organization is positively correlated with the amount of money spent and the number of employees dedicated to management of information flow? To make such an assumption would be dangerous, and likely incorrect. We must ask the question, however, why the differing patterns exist and what the patterns indicate about the value of information to the organization. It seems reasonable to assume that information technology should be integrated throughout the organization, regardless of any centralized information technology group, since the role and advantage of information technology itself is having it permeate the organization to maximize the flow of information and the exchange of ideas (Woodsworth, 1991). Though the supposition that information technology would flatten the hierarchy has been shown to be questionable, it is not debatable that information technology affects the structure, via the technology, via the skilled personnel it demands, and via the skills that the typical worker can now acquire to implement information technology (because the technology has improved even if the quality of the employee has not). Small organizations wishing to survive must keep as current as possible without negatively impacting their economic positions. This can best be achieved by flexibility and resolute attention to the mission of the organization and sensitivity to the customer base. Not to be overlooked is attention to the information itself, not just the technology. What the organization needs to know, what creative activities are ongoing, what each sector contributes and how economically viable each contribution is mean as much to the survival of the organization as does investment in the technology.

## Summary

Sometimes too much information or too much technology can decrease efficiency (McWilliams, 1995). Understanding the value to the organization of the information that flows through the channels that are enabled by the technology is critical to managing that technology to the advantage of the organization. That value of information is linked to its usefulness to the organization, and the user primarily determines information value. If information is inaccessible simply because there is too much of it, it has no value and may actually be a wasted cost due to the cost of collection, which suggests that organizations of all sizes need to evaluate the cost and benefit of information gathering. Just because it is possible to collect enormous bodies of information does not mean that it is profitable.

There are no quick and easy answers to any of the issues discussed here. Digital accessibility impacts organizational structure and the ways in which organizations gather, use, and value information in ways that we do not yet fully understand. In the present climate of rapid change in the extent and means of accessibility, determining both the nature of the changes and their impact is a challenge. The differing approaches to infusion of information technology provide a fertile field for examination of how information value changes in relation to differing structures and the extent to which those structures are a result of changes in digital accessibility. Research needs to be undertaken to determine how much flattening of the organizational hierarchy has occurred and how much of it has to do with information technology versus just changes in the social structure. Continued review and evaluation of the impact of information technology in organizations and in all aspects of society need to be conducted. We know that management structures are changing in response to the digital revolution, but so is society. The challenge is to cope with the changes in ways that will optimize the value of information to the organization, to society as a whole, and to the individuals who compose both.

## References

Anderson, C. L. and Hauptman, R. 1993. *Technology and Information Services: Challenges for the 1990s.* NJ: Ablex.

DeYoung, H. G. October 9, 1995. The Trouble with Technology. *Computerworld Premier 100.* pp. 42–43.

Earls, A. June, 1995. *An Ounce of Training . . . Computerworld 100 Best Places to Work.* pp. 51–55.

Gardner, W. L. and Peluchette, J.V.E. 1991. Computer-Mediated Communication Settings: A Self-Presentational Perspective. In E. Szewczak, C. Snodgrass, and M. Khosrowpour, (Eds.). *Management Impacts of Information Technology: Perspectives on Organizational Change and Growth* pp. 168-205. Harrisburg. PA: Idea Group.

Gerstein, M. S. 1992. From Machine Bureaucracies to Networked Organizations: An Architectural Journey. In D. A. Nadler, M. S. Gerstein, and R. B. Shaw, (Eds.). *Organization Architecture: Designs for Changing Organizations* pp. 10–38. San Francisco, CA: Josey-Bass, Inc.

Kaltnekar, Z. 1991. Information Technology and the Humanization of Work. In E. Szewczak, C. Snodgrass, and M. Khosrowpour, (Eds.). *Management Impacts of Information Technology: Perspectives on Organizational Change and Growth* pp. 493–533. Harrisburg, PA: Idea Group

Malloy, A. May 1, 1995. The Global 100 List. *Computerworld Global 100* pp. 54–63.

McWilliams, B. October 9, 1995. The Premier 100: The Most Effective Companies at Managing Information. *Computerworld Premier 100* pp. 20–25.

Nadler, D. A. 1992. Introduction: Organization Architecture: A Metaphor for Change. In D. A. Nadler, M. S. Gerstein, and R. B. Shaw, (Eds.). *Organization Architecture: Designs for Changing Organizations* pp. 1–9. San Francisco, CA: Josey-Bass, Inc.

Nadler, D. A., and Tushman, M. L. 1992. Designing Organizations that Have Good Fit: A Framework for Understanding New Architectures. In D. A. Nadler, M. S. Gerstein, and R. B. Shaw, (Eds.). *Organization Architecture: Designs for Changing Organizations* pp. 39–57. San Francisco, CA: Josey-Bass, Inc.

Rayner, B. May 1, 1995. The Global 100. *Computerworld Global 100* pp. 7–8.

Shimada, T. 1991. The Impact of Information Technology on Organizations in Japanese Companies. In E. Szewczak, C. Snodgrass, and M. Khosrowpour, (Eds.). *Management Impacts of Information Technology: Perspectives on Organizational Change and Growth* pp. 298–329. Harrisburg, PA: Idea Group.

Smithe, A. April, 1996. Instant Answers. *Windows Magazine* 7(4): 158–172.

Sweat, J. and Hibbard, J. June 21, 1999. Customer Disservice. *Information Week* pp. 65-78.

Szygenda, R. February 8, 1999. Executive Reports: Information's Competitive Edge. *InformationWeek.* [online] http://www.informationweek.com/720/gmcorp.htm

Thyfault, M. E,, Johnston, S. J., & Sweat, J. (October 5, 1998). The Service Imperative. *InformationWeek.* [online] http://www.informationweek.com/703/03iusrv.htm

Williams, J. 1991. Negative Consequences of Information Technology. In E. Szewczak, C. Snodgrass, and M. Khosrowpour, (Eds.). *Management Impacts of Information Technology: Perspectives on Organizational Change and Growth* pp. 48–75. Harrisburg, PA: Idea Group.

Woodsworth, A. 1991. *Patterns and Options for Managing Information Technology on Campus.* Chicago: ALA.

# About the Author

Melanie J. Norton is an assistant professor in the School of Library and Information Science at the University of Southern Mississippi in Hattiesburg. Her experience includes LAN development and management, and managing a university multimedia library and laboratory system. She has worked in a medical records library and in a range of government, manufacturing, and retail settings. Her research interests include information economics, information and data retrieval, and issues in the technological and human contexts of communication.

# Index

# More Books from Information Today, Inc.

## ARIST 34
### Annual Review of Information Science and Technology
**Edited by Professor Martha E. Williams**

Since 1966, the *Annual Review of Information Science and Technology (ARIST)* has been continuously at the cutting edge in contributing a useful and comprehensive view of the broad field of information science and technology. *ARIST* reviews numerous topics within the field and ultimately provides this annual source of ideas, trends, and references to the literature. Published by Information Today, Inc. on behalf of the American Society for Information Science (ASIS), *ARIST Volume 34* (1999) is the latest volume in this legendary series.

The newest edition of *ARIST* covers the following nine topics:

The History of Documentation and Information Science (Colin Burke) • Applications of Machine Learning in Information Retrieval (Sally Jo Cunningham, Jamie Littin, and Ian Witten) • Privacy and Digital Information (Philip Doty) • Cognitive Information Retrieval (Peter Ingwersen) • Text Mining (Walter Trybula) • Methodologies for Human Behavioral Research (Peiling Wang) • Measuring the Internet (Robert Williams and Bob Molyneux) • Infometric Laws (Concepcion Wilson and William Hood) • Using and Reading Scholarly Literature (Donald W. King and Carol Tenopir) • Literature Dynamics: Studies on Growth, Diffusion, and Epidemics (Albert Tabah).

*ARIST* is scholarly, thorough, up-to-date, well written, and readable by an audience that goes beyond the authors' immediate peer group to researchers and practitioners in information science and technology in general and ASIS members in particular.

**Hardbound • ISBN 1-57387-093-5**
**ASIS Members $79.95          Non-Members $99.95**

## KNOWLEDGE MANAGEMENT FOR THE INFORMATION PROFESSIONAL
**Edited by T. Kanti Srikantaiah and Michael E.D Koenig**

Written from the perspective of the information community, this book examines the business community's recent enthusiasm for "Knowledge Management." With contributions from 26 leading KM practitioners, academicians, and information professionals, editors Srikantaiah and Koenig bridge the gap between two distinct perspectives, equipping information professionals with the tools to make a broader and more effective contribution in developing KM systems and creating a knowledge management culture within their organizations.

**Hardbound • ISBN 1-57387-079-X**
**ASIS Members $35.60          Non-Members $44.50**

## INFORMATION MANAGEMENT FOR THE INTELLIGENT ORGANIZATION, 2nd Edition

### Chun Wei Choo

The intelligent organization is one that is skilled at marshalling its information resources and capabilities, transforming information into knowledge, and using this knowledge to sustain and enhance its performance in a restless environment. The objective of this newly updated and expanded book is to develop an understanding of how an organization may manage its information processes more effectively in order to achieve these goals. This book is a must read for senior managers and administrators, information managers, information specialists and practitioners, information technologists, and anyone whose work in an organization involves acquiring, creating, organizing, or using knowledge.

**Hardbound • ISBN 1-57387-057-9**
**ASIS Members $31.60          Non-Members $39.50**

## BEYOND BOOK INDEXING
### *How to Get Started in Web Indexing, Embedded Indexing, and Other Computer-Based Media*

### Edited by Marilyn Rowland and Diane Brenner

Are you curious about new indexing technologies? Would you like to develop and create innovative indexes that provide access to online resources, multimedia, or online help? Do you want to learn new skills and expand your marketing possibilities? In *Beyond Book Indexing*, edited by Diane Brenner and Marilyn Rowland, 12 articles written by 10 noted indexing professionals provide an in-depth look at current and emerging computer-based technologies and offer suggestions for obtaining work in these fields. Extensive references and a glossary round out this informative and exciting new book.

**Softbound • ISBN 1-57387-081-1 • $31.25**

## MILLENNIUM INTELLIGENCE
### *Understanding & Conducting Competitive Intelligence in the Digital Age*

### Edited by Jerry Miller

With contributions from the world's leading business intelligence practitioners, here is a tremendously informative and practical look at the CI process, how it is changing, and how it can be managed effectively in the Digital Age. Loaded with case studies, tips, and techniques, chapters include What Is Intelligence?; The Skills Needed to Execute Intelligence Effectively; Information Sources Used for Intelligence; The Legal and Ethical Aspects of Intelligence; Corporate Security and Intelligence ...and much more!

**Softbound • ISBN 0-910965-28-5 • $29.95**